FIFA WORLD CUP BOOK

This edition published in 1998 by Carlton Books Limited
20 St Anne's Court, Wardour Street, London W1V 3AW

1 3 5 7 9 10 8 6 4 2

A CIP record for this book is available from the British Library

ISBN 1 85868 440 4

Project Editors: Martin Corteel & Roland Hall
Art Editor: Zoë Maggs
Production: Sarah Schuman
Picture Research: Lorna Ainger

Printed and bound in Great Britain

FIFA WORLD CUP BOOK

KEIR RADNEDGE

CARLTON

Contents

Introduction

Vive La France, Vive Le Foot

Nothing in sport matches the World Cup. The Olympic Games may take over cities and last almost as long and just about every other sport may have world championships as well, but there is nothing like the real thing – and that begins in the dramatic, new Stade de France on Wednesday, June 10 when Brazil face Scotland. The climax follows just over four weeks later, back in the new stadium when the Final is played.

France is playing host to the World Cup finals for the second time. The first time was back in 1938, in the shadow of oncoming war. The second French finals, exactly 60 years later, take place in the happy shadow of the millennium.

The 1998 World Cup finals will thus set the tone for football going into the 21st century. The prospects could hardly be better.

In 1990 defensive play, no-goal-scoring tactics and some questionable player attitudes marked the final round of the World Cup. That was when FIFA, the world governing body, acted to breathe new life into the spirit of the game. Now three points for a win has been universally adopted, a crackdown has been undertaken by referees against the so-called "professional foul" and against time-wasting and the feigning of injury. The game has opened its mind to the value of experimentation with new ideas.

FIFA has set its face, thus far, against electronic aids to assist the referee when it comes to the ball crossing the goal-line or penalty-fringe incidents. But the assistant referees – "linesmen" no longer – now give the referee an electronic bleep as well as a waving flag when an infraction is committed.

None of the worldwide developments of the game would have been possible without the flood of television and sponsorship money. There will be around 40 companies involved in France 98 at one sponsorship level or another – from the official match ball to the official office equipment.

The World Cup will be 68 years old in France. But it remains quite as young at heart as when its pioneers made their way to Uruguay on the sporting voyage of the century back in 1930.

Paris, the inspirational capital of France, will be host to the final of football's most prestigious World Cup

Fans everywhere will be following the most popular sporting event in the world. There will be a carnival atmosphere as World Cup fever grips the planet.

ABOVE: ***Flying the flag for Norway – this fan is blinded by the team that will dominate his viewing during the World Cup in France***

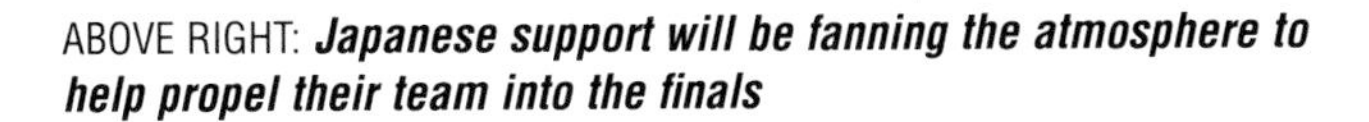

ABOVE RIGHT: ***Japanese support will be fanning the atmosphere to help propel their team into the finals***

CENTRE RIGHT: ***The African continent will be well represented in 1998 and the countries partaking in this venerable competition will not be short of enthusiastic backing***

BOTTOM RIGHT: ***No clowning around – England supporters will be out in force urging the national team to better their last World Cup efforts***

The 1998 World Cup Finals

© 1995 ISL TM

The Draw – A Festival of Football

Sepp Blatter presiding over the draw for the World Cup in France

No fewer than 32 international footballers topped the bill at the draw for the World Cup finals in Marseille on December 4 last year. Each player – one from each of the qualified nations – took a minor turn in helping the FIFA general secretary, Sepp Blatter, extract the all-important lottery numbers from the glass bowls to decide the shape of the first round groups.

But, more important, they also took to the pitch in the sensationally redeveloped Stade Velodrome for an exhibition game featuring Europe against the Rest of the World. The Rest won the match 5–2 but the result itself was the least important feature of the evening. More important was the fulfilment of a promise from the French organisers that the competition should be given back to football.

As Michel Platini, France's greatest-ever footballer and co-president of the organising committee, explained: "The draws at all the World Cups I have been to have been about displays and dancers and officials. Well, we want to put football back at the heart of the tournament – starting with the draw itself."

All the best

Platini selected the players for the match and FIFA did its best to obtain their release from their clubs. Not all the superstars selected turned out on the day. But FIFA's own Footballer of the Year, Ronaldo from Brazil, was there, and his two goals gave us a hint of the excitement to come in the finals tournament itself.

The two managers for the teams were Franz Beckenbauer for Europe and Carlos Alberto Parreira for the Rest of the World. They were appropriate choices as the last two World Cup-winning coaches and high-profile representatives of the varying football philosophies of the game's two oldest continents.

Top Ranking

Platini and organising co-president Fernand Sastre had originally planned to stage the draw at half-time in the match. But the problems of timing and television coordination eventually persuaded them, reluctantly, to switch the administrative action to the end of the match.

That was when Blatter, despite the icy temperatures, worked his usual magic to produce probably the most even draw in the finals' history.

Hosts France, holders Brazil, past winners Italy, Argentina and Germany and top-ranked European nations Spain, Holland and Romania – their status based on their records in the past three Cups as well as the world rankings – were the eight top seeds. After that the finalist nations were evenly balanced so that the nations of South America, CONCACAF, Africa and Asia were all spread evenly across the draw.

The Opening Match, as per the tradition established in 1974, features holders, this time Brazil against Scotland on June 10 at the new Stade de France in the Paris suburb of Saint-Denis.

The first round will be completed on June 26, with the top two teams in each group going through to the second round. The expansion of the finals from 24 to 32 teams means that there will be no more mathematical complications to lift any of the third-placed teams into the second round. If teams are level on points they will be separated on the basis of goal difference, then goals scored, then mutual result.

From the second round onwards, the World Cup steps up the excitement in knock-out drama. The second-round matches will be played at the rate of two per day from June 27 to 30. The quarter-finals will be on July 3 and 4 then the semi-finals at the Stade de France and in Marseille. Unlike the European Championship, FIFA retains a Third Place Play-off at the World Cup.

Eventually, the four-yearly extravaganza reaches a climax with the Final on July 12 in the Stade de France.

GROUP A	GROUP B
Brazil	Italy
Scotland	Chile
Morocco	Cameroon
Norway	Austria

GROUP C	GROUP D
Saudi Arabia	Paraguay
Denmark	Bulgaria
France	Spain
South Africa	Nigeria

GROUP E	GROUP F
South Korea	Yugoslavia
Mexico	Iran
Holland	Germany
Belgium	USA

GROUP G	GROUP H
England	Argentina
Tunisia	Japan
Romania	Jamaica
Colombia	Croatia

The Venues

Elysian Fields

All the 10 cities which will be welcoming the fans, players, officials and media of the competing nations to the 64-match tournament are important homes of domestic French soccer. The Opening Match on June 10, one semi-final and the Final itself on July 12 will be played in the one new stadum, the 80,000-capacity Stade de France being built in the St Denis suburb of the capital, Paris. The other semi-final will be staged in the historic Velodrome stadium in Marseille. Redevelopment of all the stadia was planned so that the host clubs' league and cup and European competitive programmes would not be interrupted by work.

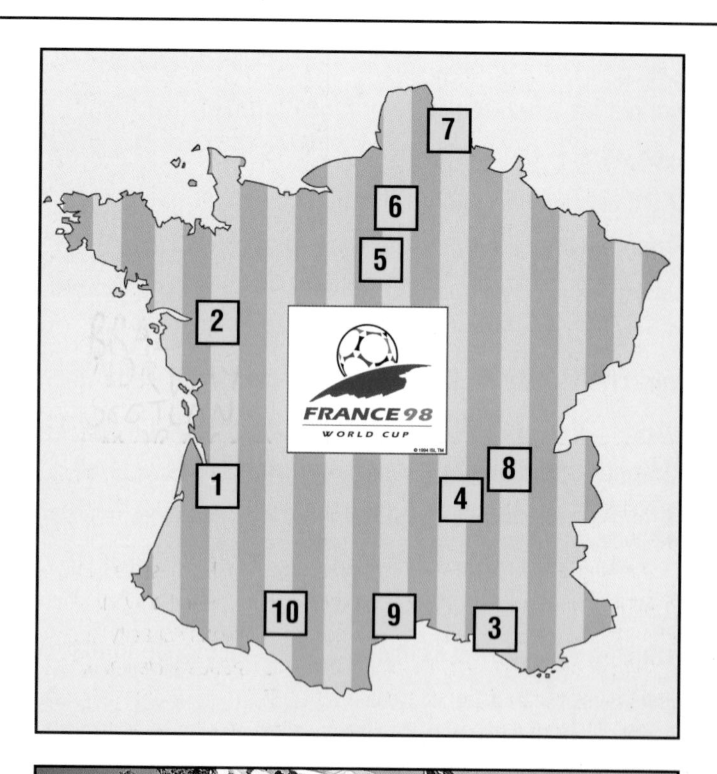

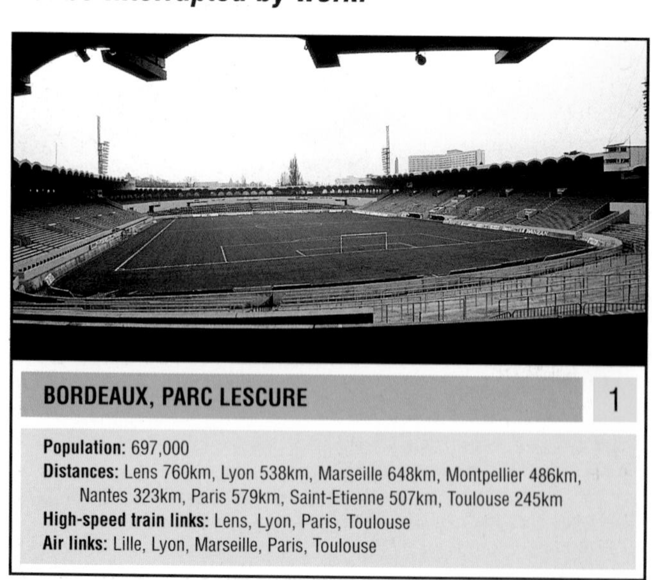

BORDEAUX, PARC LESCURE 1

Population: 697,000
Distances: Lens 760km, Lyon 538km, Marseille 648km, Montpellier 486km, Nantes 323km, Paris 579km, Saint-Etienne 507km, Toulouse 245km
High-speed train links: Lens, Lyon, Paris, Toulouse
Air links: Lille, Lyon, Marseille, Paris, Toulouse

Stadium capacity for the World Cup finals will be 35,200, all seated, with 15,000 places covered. Before the F52 million redevelopment, stadium capacity was 46,900 with 21,300 seated.

Girondins of Bordeaux, one of the greatest clubs in France, are at home in the Parc Lescure. Bordeaux have won the league championship three times and the French cup twice. In 1995–96 they achieved the remarkable feat of qualifying from the UEFA-Intertoto Cup and ultimately reaching the UEFA Cup Final where, after almost a full year of football, they lost to Bayern Munich.

NANTES, LA BEAUJOIRE 2

Population: 499,200
Distances: Bordeaux 323km, Lens 566km, Lyon 613km, Marseille 972km, Montpellier 809km, Paris 384km, Saint-Etienne 608km, Toulouse 567km
High-speed train links: Lens, Lyon, Marseille, Paris, Saint-Etienne, Toulouse
Air links: Lyon, Marseille, Montpellier, Paris

Stadium capacity for the World Cup finals will be 39,500 following the completion of a F44 million reconstruction programme. Previous ground capacity, which was built for the 1984 European Championship, was 52,000. The Beaujoire stadium is 7km from the centre of Nantes.

FC Nantes-Atlantique are one of the great success stories of modern French football. With an outstanding reputation for developing their own players, the club have won the French championship seven times and the cup once. In 1996 they reached the semi-finals of the European Champions League before losing to eventual cup-winners Juventus.

Spread out across the length and breadth of France, the 10 venues for the 1998 World Cup have been refurbished to meet the highest international standards for outdoor sporting arenas.

MARSEILLE, VELODROME 3

Population: 1,000,000
Distances: Bordeaux 648km, Lens 954km, Lyon 313km, Montpellier 166km, Nantes 972km, Paris 773km, Saint-Etienne 330km, Toulouse 404km
High-speed train links: Bordeaux, Lens, Lyon, Montpellier, Nantes, Paris, Saint-Etienne
Air links: Bordeaux, Lille, Lyon, Nantes, Paris

Stadium capacity for the World Cup finals will be 60,000 – converting the historic Stade Vélodrome into the largest of the 1998 venue stadia after the new stadium in Paris.

Lengthy and complex negotiations concerning the massive F250 million redevelopment of the Vélodrome were completed only shortly before the deadline for host city applications. Previous capacity was 46,000 but demolition and rebuilding of all four stands have enabled virtually a new stadium to be created with a 60,000 all-seater capacity.

Olympique de Marseille made history when, in 1993, they became the first French club ever to win the European Champions Cup – by defeating Italy's AC Milan in Munich. Victory was later tarnished by revelations about a match-fixing scandal in which president Bernard Tapie, several club officials and at least one player were implicated. The financial and disciplinary fall-out led to Marseille being relegated but, under new ownership, this most passionately-supported of all French clubs regained their place in the top division in 1996–97 season. Olympique de Marseille have won the French league championship nine times and the cup on 10 occasions.

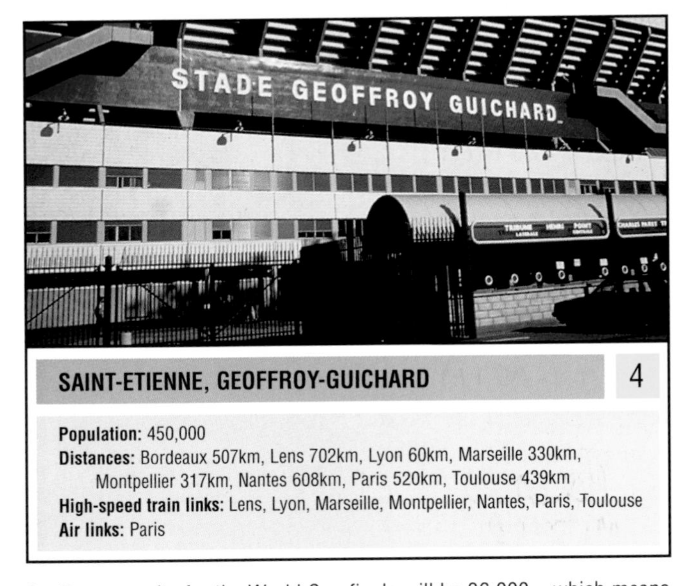

SAINT-ETIENNE, GEOFFROY-GUICHARD 4

Population: 450,000
Distances: Bordeaux 507km, Lens 702km, Lyon 60km, Marseille 330km, Montpellier 317km, Nantes 608km, Paris 520km, Toulouse 439km
High-speed train links: Lens, Lyon, Marseille, Montpellier, Nantes, Paris, Toulouse
Air links: Paris

Stadium capacity for the World Cup finals will be 36,000 – which means a reduction of 6,000 from the previous 42,000. However, implementation of a F76 million redevelopment and modernization plan means the stadium will become all-seater as required by World Cup regulations.

The Association Sportive Saint-Etienne have won the French league title 10 times and the French cup on six occasions. "Les Verts" were outstanding representatives for France in the European club competitions in the 1970s, finishing runners-up to Bayern Munich in the Champions Cup in 1976.

PARIS, PARC DES PRINCES 5

Population: 2,200,000 (9,000,000 including urban area)
Distances: Bordeaux 579km, Lens 199km, Lyon 462km, Marseille 773km, Montpellier 760km, Nantes 384km, Saint-Etienne 520km, Toulouse 698km
High-speed train links: Bordeaux, Lens, Lyon, Marseille, Montpellier, Nantes, Saint-Etienne, Toulouse

Totally rebuilt in 1972 with a 49,000 capacity, Stade du Parc des Princes is situated in a residential district of central Paris and is home to Paris Saint-Germain Football Club. The stadium staged the final of the 1984 European Championship and was used for some of the most important matches of the 1991 Rugby World Cup Finals.

Founded only 25 years ago, PSG have won the championship twice, the cup on four occasions and the European Cup-Winners' Cup in 1996, becoming the first club from the capital to win a major European prize.

The Stade de France in Saint-Denis will be the biggest stadium in France and the largest multi-function Olympic-sized stadium in the world.

PARIS, STADE DE FRANCE 6

The largest stadium in France, built in the Saint-Denis suburb and inaugurated in January this year, has a capacity of 80,000 all seated. Work began in May 1995 and was completed ahead of schedule. It is considered the largest multi-function Olympic-sized stadium anywhere in the world. The variable capacity makes it ideal as a venue for a wide range of high-attendance events and it has become the new home of the French national rugby union side as well as the football team.

Saint-Denis is 9km north of Paris. It gained fame from a bishop who, according to legend, was beheaded at Montmartre and walked, with his head under his arm, to the village which took his name. His tomb was a place of pilgrimage before becoming a royal abbey whose basilica houses 70 royal tombs.

To welcome the world, the local authority has planned an elaborate programme including a grand carnival procession, son-et-lumière, rock concert, street exhibition tracing the history of football and dance cafes along the canal.

LENS, FELIX BOLLAERT 7

Population: 376,700
Distances: Bordeaux 760km, Lyon 644km, Marseille 954km, Montpellier 941km, Nantes 566km, Paris 199km, Saint-Etienne 702km, Toulouse 880km.
High-speed train links: Bordeaux, Lyon, Marseille, Montpellier, Nantes, Paris, Saint-Etienne, Toulouse
Air links (from Lille): Bordeaux, Lyon, Marseille, Montpellier, Toulouse

Stadium capacity for the World Cup finals will be 42,000 all seated. Redevelopment has included improving access to the main stands, a new sound system, lighting and scoreboards. The Stade Bollaert, opened originally in 1932, is 10 minutes from the city centre. Racing Club de Lens, the local team, were founded in 1906. They have never won a major championship or cup but were three times runners-up in the league and twice losing cup finalists. Lens won the second division championship on three occasions. Outstanding players of the past have included Cameroon's 1990 World Cup hero, François Omam Biyik.

From June 10 to July 12, hundreds of thousands of fans will be watching the games – and travelling hundreds of kilometres around France to attend them.

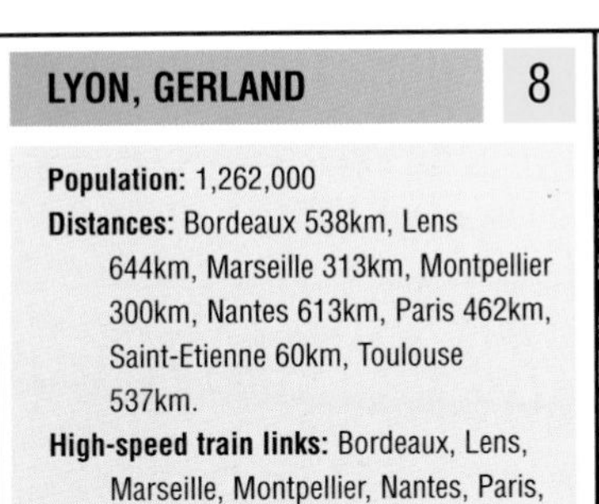

LYON, GERLAND 8

Population: 1,262,000
Distances: Bordeaux 538km, Lens 644km, Marseille 313km, Montpellier 300km, Nantes 613km, Paris 462km, Saint-Etienne 60km, Toulouse 537km.
High-speed train links: Bordeaux, Lens, Marseille, Montpellier, Nantes, Paris, Saint-Etienne, Toulouse
Air links: Bordeaux, Lille, Marseille, Nantes, Paris, Toulouse

Stadium capacity for the World Cup finals will be 44,000 all seated. The Gerland, officially listed as a historic monument, was opened in 1926. It has been extensively redesigned on all four sides with the installation of individual seating and new luxury boxes for fans plus improved dressing room facilities for the players.

Olympique Lyonnais are the host club. They have never won the French championship but carried off the cup three times, in 1964, 1967 and 1973. They have been runners-up three times and league cup runners-up in 1996. In 1964 they reached the European Cup-winners' Cup semi-finals.

MONTPELLIER, LA MOSSON 9

Population: 350,000
Distances: Bordeaux 486km, Lens 941km, Lyon 300km, Marseille 166km, Nantes 809km, Paris 760km, Saint-Etienne 317km, Toulouse 241km.
High-speed train links: Bordeaux, Lens, Lyon, Marseille, Paris, Saint-Etienne.
Air links: Lille, Nantes, Paris

Stadium capacity for the World Cup finals will be 35,500 for one of the most modern grounds in France – built in 1988 in the Paillade suburb, about 4km from the city centre. Improvements for the World Cup include new lighting, sound, scoreboard and video security systems.

The Montpellier-Hérault Sport Club is a modern success story. The present club was founded only in 1974, gaining promotion to the top division in 1981 and then again in 1987. They won the French cup in 1990 and were runners-up in 1994, also winning the League Cup in 1992. Star players have included France's Laurent Blanc and Eric Cantona.

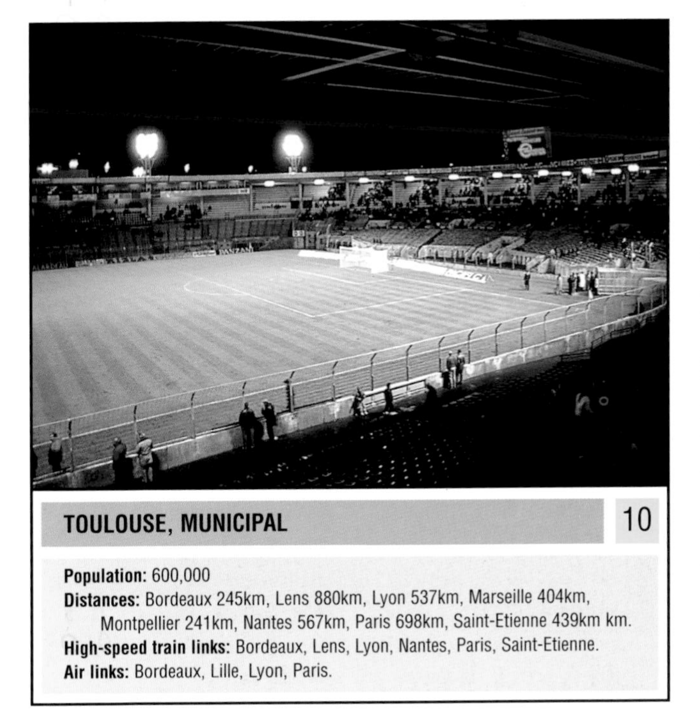

TOULOUSE, MUNICIPAL 10

Population: 600,000
Distances: Bordeaux 245km, Lens 880km, Lyon 537km, Marseille 404km, Montpellier 241km, Nantes 567km, Paris 698km, Saint-Etienne 439km km.
High-speed train links: Bordeaux, Lens, Lyon, Nantes, Paris, Saint-Etienne.
Air links: Bordeaux, Lille, Lyon, Paris.

Capacity for the World Cup finals will be 37,500, all seated, in the municipal stadium which was built in 1949 on an island between two branches of the Garonne river. The stadium, used by both local association and rugby football clubs, is close to the city centre.

Toulouse Football Club was founded in 1937, won the French cup in 1957 and were league championship runners-up in 1955. After three years in the second division, the club regained top division status last year under the managerial guidance of Alain Giresse, one of France's World Cup heroes in Spain in 1982.

The Fixtures

Chart the progress of the World Cup on these two pages, so that at the end you will have a record of the vital happenings of the tournament.

In the First Round, there are eight groups, from which the first two in each group proceed to the Last Sixteen. Space has been allocated for you to fill in the scores of the matches and the final placings in each group.

From the Last Sixteen onwards, the competition is based on a knock-out system. The teams will not be known until after the First Round is completed, but we indicate which group winners will play when and where – all the way through from the Last Sixteen to the Final. Space has again been provided for you to fill in the teams and scores for each match, as well as the goalscorers for the Final itself. Please note that all kick-off times are local.

FIRST ROUND

GROUP A

Date	Venue	Fixture	Score
June 10 (17.30)	Paris St Denis	Brazil vs. Scotland	2-1
June 10 (21.00)	Montpellier	Morocco vs. Norway	2-2
June 16 (17.30)	Bordeaux	Scotland vs. Norway	1-1
June 16 (21.00)	Nantes	Brazil vs. Morocco	4-0
June 23 (21.00)	St Etienne	Scotland vs. Morocco	0-2
June 23 (21.00)	Marseille	Brazil vs. Norway	1-4

GROUP A FINAL TABLE

Team	P	W	D	L	F	A	Pts
1 BRAZIL							
2 NORWAY							
3 SCOTLAND							
4 MOROCCO							

GROUP B

Date	Venue	Fixture	Score
June 11 (17.30)	Bordeaux	Italy vs. Chile	2-2
June 11 (21.00)	Toulouse	Cameroon vs. Austria	1-1
June 17 (17.30)	St Etienne	Chile vs. Austria	1-1
June 17 (21.00)	Montpellier	Italy vs. Cameroon	2-0
June 23 (16.00)	Nantes	Chile vs. Cameroon	2-0
June 23 (16.00)	Paris St Denis	Italy vs. Austria	2-0

GROUP B FINAL TABLE

Team	P	W	D	L	F	A	Pts
1 ITALY							
2 CHILE							
3 AUSTRIA							
4 CAMEROON							

GROUP C

Date	Venue	Fixture	Score
June 12 (17.30)	Lens	Saudi Arabia vs. Denmark	0-1
June 12 (21.00)	Marseille	France vs. South Africa	3-0
June 18 (17.30)	Toulouse	South Africa vs. Denmark	....–.....
June 18 (21.00)	Paris St Denis	France vs. Saudi Arabia	....–.....
June 24 (16.00)	Bordeaux	S Africa vs. Saudi Arabia	....–.....
June 24 (16.00)	Lyon	France vs. Denmark	....–.....

GROUP C FINAL TABLE

Team	P	W	D	L	F	A	Pts
1 FRANCE							
2 DENMARK							
3 SAUDI ARABIA							
4 SOUTH AFRICA							

GROUP D

Date	Venue	Fixture	Score
June 12 (14.30)	Montpellier	Paraguay vs. Bulgaria	0-0
June 13 (14.30)	Nantes	Spain vs. Nigeria	2-3
June 19 (17.30)	Paris	Nigeria vs. Bulgaria	....–.....
June 19 (21.00)	St Etienne	Spain vs. Paraguay	....–.....
June 24 (21.00)	Toulouse	Nigeria vs. Paraguay	....–.....
June 24 (21.00)	Lens	Spain vs. Bulgaria	....–.....

GROUP D FINAL TABLE

Team	P	W	D	L	F	A	Pts
1 NIGERIA							
2 PARAGUAY							
3 SPAIN							
4 BULGARIA							

GROUP E

Date	Venue	Fixture	Score
June 13 (17.30)	Lyon	South Korea vs. Mexico	1-3
June 13 (21.00)	Paris St Denis	Holland vs. Belgium	0-0
June 20 (17.30)	Bordeaux	Belgium vs. Mexico	....–.....
June 20 (21.00)	Marseille	Holland vs. South Korea	....–.....
June 25 (16.00)	Paris	Belgium vs. South Korea	....–.....
June 25 (16.00)	St Etienne	Holland vs. Mexicio	....–.....

GROUP E FINAL TABLE

Team	P	W	D	L	F	A	Pts
1 HOLLAND							
2 MEXICO							
3 BELGIUM							
4 SOUTH KOREA							

GROUP F

Date	Venue	Fixture	Score
June 14 (17.30)	St Etienne	Yugoslavia vs. Iran	1-0
June 15 (21.00)	Paris	Germany vs. USA	2-0
June 21 (14.30)	Lens	Germany vs. Yugoslavia	....–.....
June 21 (21.00)	Lyons	USA vs. Iran	....–.....
June 25 (21.00)	Nantes	USA vs. Yugoslavia	....–.....
June 25 (21.00)	Montpellier	Germany vs. Iran	....–.....

GROUP F FINAL TABLE

Team	P	W	D	L	F	A	Pts
1 GERMANY							
2 YUGOSLAVIA							
3 IRAN							
4 USA							

GROUP G

Date	Venue	Fixture	Score
June 15 (14.30)	Marseille	**England vs. Tunisia**	2–0
June 15 (17.30)	Lyon	**Romania vs. Colombia**	1–0
June 22 (17.30)	Montpellier	**Colombia vs. Tunisia**	.....–.....
June 22 (21.00)	Toulouse	**Romania vs. England**	.....–.....
June 26 (21.00)	Lens	**Colombia vs. England**	.....–.....
June 26 (21.00)	Paris St Denis	**Romania vs. Tunisia**	.....–.....

GROUP G FINAL TABLE

Team	P	W	D	L	F	A	Pts
1 ROMANIA	......	......	......	......	......	......	......
2 ENGLAND	......	......	......	......	......	......	......
3 COLOMBIA	......	......	......	......	......	......	......
4 TUNISIA	......	......	......	......	......	......	......

GROUP H

Date	Venue	Fixture	Score
June 14 (14.30)	Toulouse	**Argentina vs. Japan**	1–0
June 14 (21.00)	Lens	**Jamaica vs. Croatia**	1–3
June 20 (14.30)	Nantes	**Japan vs. Croatia**	.....–.....
June 21 (17.30)	Paris	**Argentina vs. Jamaica**	.....–.....
June 26 (16.00)	Lyon	**Japan vs. Jamaica**	.....–.....
June 26 (16.00)	Bordeaux	**Argentina vs. Croatia**	.....–.....

GROUP H FINAL TABLE

Team	P	W	D	L	F	A	Pts
1 ARGENTINA	......	......	......	......	......	......	......
2 CROATIA	......	......	......	......	......	......	......
3 JAMAICA	......	......	......	......	......	......	......
4 JAPAN	......	......	......	......	......	......	......

LAST SIXTEEN

June 27, Parc des Princes (21.00)
Winner Group A vs. Runner-up of Group B
BRAZIL 4 - 1 CHILE

June 27, Marseille (16.30)
Winner of Group B vs. Runner-up of Group A
ITALY 2 - 0 NORWAY

June 28, Paris St Denis (21.00)
Winner of Group D vs. Runner-up of Group C
NIGERIA 1 - 4 DENMARK

June 28, Lens (16.30)
Winner of Group C vs. Runner-up of Group D
FRANCE 1 - 0 PARAGUAY

June 29, Toulouse (21.00)
Winner of Group E vs. Runner-up of Group F
HOLLAND 1 - 0 YUGOSLAVIA

June 29, Montpellier (16.30)
Winner of Group F vs. Runner-up of Group E
GERMANY 2 - 1 MEXICO

June 30, St Etienne (21.00)
Winner of Group H vs. Runner-up of Group G
ARGENTINA 2 - 2 ENGLAND (4 - 3 PENS)

June 30, Bordeaux (16.30)
Winner of Group G vs. Runner-up of Group H
ROMANIA 1 - 2 CROATIA

QUARTER-FINALS

July 3, Paris St Denis (16.30)
Winner in Marseille vs. Winner in Lens
ITALY 0 - 0 FRANCE (4 - 3 PENS)

July 3, Nantes (21.00)
Winner in Parc des Princes vs. Winner in Paris St Denis
BRAZIL 3 - 2 DENMARK

July 4, Marseille (16.30)
Winner in Toulouse vs. Winner in St Etienne
HOLLAND 2 - 1 ARGENTINA

July 4, Lyon (21.00)
Winner in Montpellier vs. Winner in Bordeaux
GERMANY 0 - 3 CROATIA

SEMI-FINALS

July 7, Marseille (21.00)
Winner of Nantes quarter-final vs. Winner of Marseille quarter-final
BRAZIL 1 - 1 HOLLAND (4 - 2 PENS)

July 8, Paris St Denis (21.00)
Winner of Paris St Denis quarter-final vs. Winner of Lyon quarter-final
FRANCE 2 - 1 CROATIA

THIRD/FOURTH PLACE PLAY-OFF

July 11, Paris St Denis (21.00)
HOLLAND 1 - 2 CROATIA

FINAL

July 12, Paris St Denis (21.00)

Result
FRANCE 3 - 0 BRAZIL

Scorers
ZIDANE x2 PETIT

Scorers

How They Qualified

The Road to France

The 180 national teams that started down the road to qualification for France 98 were whittled down to 32 by December 1997. 643 games were played to decide who would get to battle on the playing fields of France for the honour of becoming World Champions of football. Only one in every five of those games was a draw, and the goal scoring average was nearly three per game. In total 1,922 goals were scored along the way. One of the most significant was by Japan, who became the first team in the history of the World Cup to qualify with a golden goal, in their play-off game against Iran. France and Brazil qualified automatically, as hosts and holders respectively, but the competition for the 30 other places was fierce. With five African countries in the final draw, places for European teams were hotly contested. After years of preliminary rounds, the teams were put into final groups to fight for the right to come to France. Here are the final group standings from when the final whistle was eventually blown in the last game after more than 950 hours of world-class football qualification. There were surprises, upsets and celebrations, winners and losers, but rest assured that every team that takes the field in the summer of 1998 in France has earned its place.

EUROPE

EUROPE GROUP ONE

Team	*P*	*W*	*D*	*L*	*F*	*A*	*Pts*
Denmark	8	5	2	1	14	6	17
Croatia*	8	4	3	1	17	12	15
Greece	8	4	2	2	11	4	14
Bosnia-Herzegovina	8	3	0	5	9	14	9
Slovenia	8	0	1	7	5	20	1

* Qualified after play-off

EUROPE GROUP TWO

Team	*P*	*W*	*D*	*L*	*F*	*A*	*Pts*
England	8	6	1	1	15	2	19
Italy*	8	5	3	0	11	1	18
Poland	8	3	1	4	10	12	10
Georgia	8	3	1	4	7	9	10
Moldova	8	0	0	8	2	21	0

* Qualified after play-off

EUROPE GROUP THREE

Team	*P*	*W*	*D*	*L*	*F*	*A*	*Pts*
Norway	8	6	2	0	21	2	20
Hungary	8	3	3	2	10	8	12
Finland	8	3	2	3	11	12	11
Switzerland	8	3	1	4	11	12	10
Azerbaijan	8	1	0	7	3	22	3

EUROPE GROUP FOUR

Team	*P*	*W*	*D*	*L*	*F*	*A*	*Pts*
Austria	10	8	1	1	17	4	25
Scotland	10	7	2	1	15	3	23
Sweden	10	7	0	3	16	9	21
Latvia	10	3	1	6	10	14	10
Estonia	10	1	1	8	4	16	4
Belarus	10	1	1	8	5	21	4

EUROPE GROUP FIVE

Team	*P*	*W*	*D*	*L*	*F*	*A*	*Pts*
Bulgaria	8	6	0	2	18	9	18
Russia	8	5	2	1	19	5	17
Israel	8	4	1	3	9	7	13
Cyprus	8	3	1	4	10	15	10
Luxembourg	8	0	0	8	2	22	0

EUROPE GROUP SIX

Team	*P*	*W*	*D*	*L*	*F*	*A*	*Pts*
Spain	10	8	2	0	26	6	26
Yugoslavia*	10	7	2	1	29	7	23
Czech Republic	10	5	1	4	16	6	16
Slovakia	10	5	1	4	18	14	16
Faroe Islands	10	2	0	8	10	31	6
Malta	10	0	0	10	2	37	0

* Qualified after play-off

EUROPE GROUP SEVEN

Team	*P*	*W*	*D*	*L*	*F*	*A*	*Pts*
Netherlands	8	6	1	1	26	4	19
Belgium*	8	6	0	2	20	11	18
Turkey	8	4	2	2	21	9	14
Wales	8	2	1	5	20	21	7
San Marino	8	0	0	8	0	42	0

* Qualified after play-off

EUROPE GROUP EIGHT

Team	*P*	*W*	*D*	*L*	*F*	*A*	*Pts*
Romania	10	9	1	0	37	4	28
Republic of Ireland	10	5	3	2	22	8	18
Lithuania	10	5	2	8	11	8	17
FYR Macedonia	10	4	1	5	22	18	13
Iceland	10	2	3	5	11	16	9
Liechtenstein	10	0	0	10	3	52	0

EUROPE GROUP NINE

Team	*P*	*W*	*D*	*L*	*F*	*A*	*Pts*
Germany	10	6	4	0	23	9	22
Ukraine	10	6	2	2	10	6	20
Portugal	10	5	4	1	12	4	19
Armenia	10	1	5	4	8	17	8
Northern Ireland	10	1	4	5	6	10	7
Albania	10	1	1	8	7	20	4

EUROPEAN PLAY-OFFS

Aggregate Scores

Italy 2–1 Russia
Yugoslavia 12–1 Hungary
Belgium 3–2 Republic of Ireland
Croatia 3–1 Ukraine

Thirty-two teams have come a long way since the first qualifiers.

THE AMERICAS

SOUTH AMERICA

Team	*P*	*W*	*D*	*L*	*F*	*A*	*Pts*
Argentina	16	8	6	2	23	13	30
Paraguay	16	9	2	5	21	14	29
Colombia	16	8	4	4	23	15	28
Chile	16	7	4	5	32	18	25
Peru	16	7	4	5	19	20	25
Ecuador	16	6	3	7	22	21	21
Uruguay	16	6	3	7	18	21	21
Bolivia	16	4	5	7	18	21	17
Venezuela	16	0	3	13	8	41	3

CONCACAF

Team	*P*	*W*	*D*	*L*	*F*	*A*	*Pts*
Mexico	10	4	6	0	23	7	18
United States	10	4	5	1	17	9	17
Jamaica	10	3	5	2	17	12	14
Costa Rica	10	3	3	4	13	12	12
El Salvador	10	2	4	4	11	16	10
Canada	10	1	3	6	5	20	6

ASIA

ASIA GROUP A

Team	*P*	*W*	*D*	*L*	*F*	*A*	*Pts*
Saudi Arabia	8	4	2	2	8	6	14
Iran*	8	3	3	2	13	8	12
China	8	3	2	3	11	14	11
Qatar	8	3	1	4	7	10	10
Kuwait	8	3	2	4	7	8	8

* Qualified after play-off

ASIA GROUP B

Team	*P*	*W*	*D*	*L*	*F*	*A*	*Pts*
South Korea	8	6	1	1	19	7	19
Japan*	8	3	4	1	17	9	13
United Arab Emirates	8	2	3	3	9	12	9
Uzbekistan	8	1	3	4	13	18	6
Kazakhstan	8	1	3	4	7	19	6

* Qualified after play-off

ASIA-OCEANIA PLAY-OFF

Aggregate Scores

Iran* 3–3 Australia

*Iran qualified on the away goals rule

STATISTICS

TOP SCORERS ...

Player	*Country*	*Goal count*
Mijatovic	Yugoslavia	14 goals in 12 games (average 1.17 per game)
Bagheri	Iran	19 goals in 17 games (average 1.12 per game)
Zamorano	Mexico	12 goals in 16 games (average 0.75 per game)

AFRICA

AFRICA GROUP ONE

Team	*P*	*W*	*D*	*L*	*F*	*A*	*Pts*
Nigeria	6	4	1	1	10	4	13
Guinea	6	4	0	2	10	5	12
Kenya	6	3	1	2	11	12	10
Burkina Faso	6	0	0	6	7	17	0

AFRICA GROUP TWO

Team	*P*	*W*	*D*	*L*	*F*	*A*	*Pts*
Tunisia	6	5	1	0	10	1	16
Egypt	6	3	1	2	15	5	10
Liberia	6	1	1	4	2	10	4
Namibia	6	1	1	4	6	17	4

AFRICA GROUP THREE

Team	*P*	*W*	*D*	*L*	*F*	*A*	*Pts*
South Africa	6	4	1	1	7	3	13
Congo	6	3	1	2	5	5	10
Zambia	6	2	2	2	7	6	8
Congo DR	6	0	2	4	4	9	2

AFRICA GROUP FOUR

Team	*P*	*W*	*D*	*L*	*F*	*A*	*Pts*
Cameroon	6	4	2	0	10	4	14
Angola	6	2	4	0	7	4	10
Zimbabwe	6	1	1	4	6	7	4
Togo	6	1	1	4	6	14	4

AFRICA GROUP FIVE

Team	*P*	*W*	*D*	*L*	*F*	*A*	*Pts*
Morocco	6	5	1	0	14	2	16
Sierra Leone	5	2	1	2	4	6	7
Ghana	6	1	3	2	7	7	6
Gabon	6	0	1	4	1	11	1

STATISTICS

TOTAL NUMBER OF ...

Teams	170
Matches	643
Goals	1,922 (average 2.99 per game)
Spectators	15,205,401 (average 23,648 per game)

TOP SUPPORTERS

Country	*Attendance*	*Match*	*Date*
Iran	120,000	Iran vs. Saudi Arabia	19.9.97
Mexico	115,000	Mexico vs. Jamaica	16.10.96
Ukraine	85,000	Ukraine vs. Northern Ireland	2.4.97

BRAZIL

Only a fifth victory will be enough

Group A

Brazil are the No. 1 football nation. The only country to have won the World Cup four times. The reigning champions. The country whose national team have virtually sealed in stone the leadership of the FIFA monthly rankings. Can they do it again?

Brazil got a taste of the conditions in France at Le Tournoi in 1997

Denilson is Brazil's new hero, a lanky, coltish attacking midfielder who created a sensation at Le Tournoi de France last summer. Such a sensation, indeed, that Betis of Spain outbid Real Madrid and Barcelona and concluded a transfer option worth a world record-crunching £23 million – assuming Denilson fulfils his potential at the World Cup finals.

But it is at the apex of their attack that Brazil will be the most feared opposition at France 98. The reason is summed up in one name: Ronaldo.

A host of top prizes

From Cruzeiro in Brazil to PSV Eindhoven in Holland, to Barcelona in Spain and now with Internazionale in Italy, the name Ronaldo means the same the world over: goals, goals and more goals.

Ronaldo will be only 21 when the finals kick off, yet he has already collected the sort of accolades which usually come to players much further down the line, such as FIFA's World Footballer of the Year title and a host of other prizes and awards.

He was 34-goal top scorer in 1996–97 in Spain and added Barcelona's penalty winner in the European Cup-winners Cup Final.

Now Ronaldo is the kingpin in an astonishingly skilful team. As Internazionale of Milan president Massimo Moratti says: "He is like three players in one. It doesn't matter which direction he is facing, or how the ball is delivered to him. He can control with head, chest, thigh or foot and turn in an instant. He can convert dead-end phases of play into goals."

That's why Brazil are favourites to win a fifth World Cup.

World Cup Record

1930 finals 1st round
1934 finals 1st rnd
1938 third place
1950 runners-up
1954 quarter-finals
1958 champions
1962 champions
1966 finals 1st rnd
1970 champions
1974 4th place
1978 3rd place
1982 finals 2nd rnd
1986 quarter-finals
1990 finals 2nd rnd
1994 champions

The Coach

Mario Lobo Zagallo
Career: played for America, Flamengo and Botafogo; coached in Brazil, Kuwait, Saudi Arabia and guided Brazil to World Cup victory in 1970 and fourth place in 1974. The first man to win the World Cup as player and manager.
Born: August 9, 1931
Appointed: August 1994

Star Performers

Roberto Carlos
Position: leftback
Club: Real Madrid (Spain)
Born: April 10, 1973

Denilson
Position: midfielder
Club: Corinthians Sao Paulo
Born: August 24, 1977

Leonardo
Position: midfield
Club: Milan (Italy)
Born: September 5, 1969

Romario
Position: striker
Club: Valencia (Spain)
Born: January 29, 1986

Ronaldo
Position: centre-forward
Club: Internazionale (Italy)
Born: September 12, 1976

Roberto Carlos is one of the world's best defenders

SCOTLAND

Time to make progress

Group A

Scotland rarely fail to qualify for the World Cup finals – a remarkable feat for such a small country – but their problem has been progressing beyond Round One. They have never done so in all of their seven previous finals.

Scotland's World Cup misery is a tale of lost confidence and anti-climax familiar not only at national team but also at club level. Rangers and Celtic have dominated the Scottish game, but all they have to show on an international stage is one trophy apiece. Even Aberdeen, in the remote Highlands, can boast as much silverware.

Scotland's general international path has matched that of England. They met in the world's first international (a 0–0 draw in Glasgow) in 1872, quit FIFA and the competitive scene together in the 1920s, and returned together in 1946.

At the World Cup finals, controversy pursued them – as in 1978 when Willie Johnston tested positive in a dope check and was sent home in disgrace.

Scotland scored a memorable victory over Holland in their final group match with the help of a superb goal by Archie Gemmill, but Ally MacLeod's managerial reputation never recovered from the overall sense of failure that followed their 3–1 defeat against Peru in the opening match.

One team in Tallinn

Qualifying for France appeared possible with Sweden and Austria the main rivals in a group that could have been a lot worse. But the group will be remembered not so much for the matches which took place as for the one which did not.

October 9, 1996 was the day when the ever-loyal Scotland supporters had every reason in the World Cup to chant: "There's only one team in Tallinn ..." After a row over the quality of the floodlights, FIFA had ordered the kick-off to be brought forward from evening to midday. The Estonians failed to turn up and Scotland formally kicked off before the match was abandoned seconds later in farcical circumstances. Scotland were awarded the points but later FIFA decided to order a replay on neutral territory in Monaco which ended in a 0–0 draw. In the event, the "loss" of those two points could have proved costly. Although Scotland drew 0–0 and won 2–0 against Austria and balanced out against Sweden – winning 1–0, losing 2–1 – the group went right to the last-round wire. In the last round of matches, held in October 1997, Austria thrashed Belarus 4–0 to assure themselves of top spot in the group, but Scotland's 2–0 victory over Latvia assured them of a World Cup place by dint of finishing the European Zone as the best placed runners-up.

So once again, Scotland have reached the finals. Perhaps this time, the team won't be returning home on the first available flight after the completion of Round One.

Scotland are regular qualifiers for the finals but have yet to advance beyond Round One

World Cup Record

1930	did not enter	**1966**	did not qualify
1934	did not enter	**1970**	did not qualify
1938	did not enter	**1974**	finals 1st round
1950	qualified but withdrew	**1978**	finals 1st round
		1982	finals 1st round
1954	finals 1st round	**1986**	finals 1st round
1958	finals 1st round	**1990**	finals 1st round
1962	did not qualify	**1994**	did not qualify

The Coach

Craig Brown
Career: played for Dundee; was assistant manager at Motherwell, then manager of Clyde, and became assistant to Scotland coach Andy Roxburgh in 1986.
Born: July 1, 1940
Appointed: July 1993

Star Performers

Colin Hendry
Position: central defender
Club: Blackburn Rovers (England)
Born: December 7, 1965

Gary McAllister
Position: midfield
Club: Coventry City (England)
Born: December 25, 1964

Paul Lambert
Position: midfield
Club: Celtic
Born: August 7, 1969

John Collins
Position: midfield
Club: Monaco (France)
Born: January 31, 1968

Kevin Gallacher
Position: forward
Club: Blackburn Rovers (England)
Born: January 23, 1966

The Road to the Finals

Austria 0–0 Scotland	Scotland 2–0 Austria
Latvia 0–2 Scotland	Sweden 2–1 Scotland
Scotland 1–0 Sweden	Belarus 0–1 Scotland
Estonia 0–0 Scotland	Scotland 4–1 Belarus
Scotland 2–0 Estonia	Scotland 2–0 Latvia

MOROCCO

Worth a place at the feast

Group A

Only one nation from Africa has ever seriously challenged for the right to host the World Cup finals. That nation is Morocco. They went closer than anyone thought possible to beating the United States for the right to welcome the world in 1994. Now, if they cannot stage the finals, at least Moroccans have earned the satisfaction of being worthy to be present at the four-yearly feast.

Morocco qualified for the World Cup finals for the first time in 1970, albeit thanks to the toss of the coin when a replay against Tunisia in Marseille ended 2–2 after extra time (penalty shoot-outs not then having been introduced into the World Cup).

In the finals in Mexico the part-timers lost only 2–1 to West Germany – after leading at half-time – and forced a 1–1 draw with Bulgaria. In between they lost 3–0 to Peru, but were far from disgraced. Indeed, the only surprise is that Morocco have reached the finals on only two other occasions, 1986 and 1994.

In their second finals, also in Mexico, the Moroccans topped their first-round group ahead of England, Poland and Portugal. Then they stretched the Germans once again, and only an 89th-minute goal from Matthaus and the brilliance of goal-keeper Schumacher ended the dream.

Four years ago, at USA '94, Morocco were present again but lacked sparkle and were among the early departures after finishing bottom of Group F following defeats by Belgium, Saudi Arabia and Holland.

Surprisingly, Morocco have won the African Nations Cup only once, in 1976, but their clubs always feature strongly in the continental competitions and the Champions Cup has been carried off by Moroccan teams such as FAR Rabat and WAC Casablanca.

At USA '94 Morocco suffered from a lack of top-level international experience because most of their players – with the notable exceptions of Mohamed Chaouch from Nice and Mustafa El-Haddaoui from Angers – were home-based.

This time it will be different, not least because the nucleus of the team developed by Frenchman Henri Michel had their first taste of World Cup action at the 1994 finals in the US. Since then, players such as Nourredine Naybet , Abdelkrim El Hadriou, Rachid Azzouzi and Mustapha Hadji have matured into outstanding performers.

Morocco opened their campaign for 1998 with a 4–0 win over Sierra Leone in November 1996 and never looked back until a 1–0 home win over Ghana last June secured their place in the finals, and a small piece of history for the manager. Barring accidents, Michel will be the first Frenchman to manage at three World Cup finals – with France in 1986, Cameroon in 1994 and now Morocco.

Morocco have qualified for three previous finals, but will be hoping to improve their record

World Cup Record

1930	did not enter	**1970**	finals 1st rnd
1934	did not enter	**1974**	did not qualify
1938	did not enter	**1978**	did not qualify
1950	did not enter	**1982**	did not qualify
1954	did not enter	**1986**	finals 2nd rnd
1958	did not enter	**1990**	did not qualify
1962	did not qualify	**1994**	finals 1st rnd
1966	did not enter		

The Coach

Henri Michel
Career: played for Nantes (France); coached Nantes and the French Olympic and national teams, Paris St-Germain, Cameroon.
Born: October 29, 1947
Appointed: October 1995

Star Performers

El Brazi
Position: goalkeeper
Club: FAR
Born: March 4, 1965

Nourredine Naybet
Position: central defender
Club: La Coruna (Spain)
Born: February 10, 1970

Abdelkrim El Hadriou
Position: full-back
Club: Benfica (Portugal)
Born: March 16, 1972

Mustapha Hadji
Position: midfield
Club: Sporting Clube (Portugal)
Born: November 16, 1971

Rachid Azzouzi
Position: midfield
Club: Fortuna Koln (Germany)
Born: January 10, 1971

The Road to the Finals

Morocco 4–0 Sierra Leone
Ghana 2–2 Morocco
Gabon 0–4 Morocco
Sierra Leone 0–1 Morocco
Morocco 1–0 Ghana
Morocco 2–0 Gabon

NORWAY

Making a new name

Group A

Five days in September last year will go down as perhaps the most glorious in Norway's modern football history.

Norway before their return match against Scandinavian rivals Finland, a game won 4–0

On September 6, Norway sealed their place in the World Cup finals with a 1–0 victory in Azerbaijan. Then, on September 10, they thrashed Switzerland – expected to be their toughest rivals – 5–0 in Oslo.

Qualification vindicated the methods and disciplines imposed by manager Egil Olsen, and was further proof of football's rise in a corner of Scandinavia which used to look to the more snow-bound of winter sports for international headlines.

Norway thus appear in the finals for the second time in succession and the third in all, believing that the European venue and four years' more experience will help them improve on USA '94. Then Norway began promisingly with a 1–0 win over Mexico – the goal scored by Kjetil Rekdal, still a key man – but lost a dramatic match against Italy by the same margin and drew 0–0 against the Irish Republic.

Four points might have been enough to send Norway into the second round in most groups. Unfortunately, not only had all four teams in Group E finished on four points, but they all had a nil goal difference. Mexico, Ireland and Italy went through on goals scored, and Norway, with only one goal to celebrate, finished bottom.

Their departure was not a cause of depression among the critics. The pressure exerted by their mere presence at the finals had forced Norway into a defence-dominated mind-set. Even when Italy were reduced to 10 men after 22 minutes, they could not summon the nerve and drive to press home their numerical superiority.

Now Norway can put the record straight about the strengths they offer the world game. After all, they qualified for the finals, and Scandinavian neighbours Finland and Sweden didn't. Norway had been seen as a pale clone of the Swedes, known for their strength and commitment but lacking in technical and tactical knowhow.

Playing away

Perceptions began to alter when Norway outplayed England twice in 1994 World Cup qualifying ties, and Roseborg Trondheim scored a coup when they knocked Milan out of the 1996–97 UEFA Champions League.

Sweeper Rune Bratseth, anchor of the 1994 side, starred in Germany with Werder Bremen before retiring to a managerial post at Rosenborg. Goalkeeper Erik Thorstvedt at Tottenham was one of the first to make his mark in England, and was soon followed by a flood of players including Henning Berg, Oyvind Leonhardsen, Stig-Inge Bjornebye, Stale Solbakken and Ole Gunnar Solskjaer.

Solbakken was Norway's top scorer in the qualifying matches with four goals. They ended the campaign as one of five unbeaten European nations – in prestigious company beside Spain, Germany, Italy and Romania.

World Cup Record

1930 did not enter
1934 finals 1st round
1938 did not enter
1950 did not enter
1954 did not enter
1958 did not enter
1962 did not qualify
1966 did not qualify
1970 did not qualify
1974 did not qualify
1978 did not qualify
1982 did not qualify
1986 did not qualify
1990 did not qualify
1994 finals 1st round

The Coach

Egil Olsen
Career: played for Ostsiden, Sarpsborg, Valerengen and Frigg; coached Lyn Oslo, then the national under-21 and Olympic teams.
Born: April 22, 1942
Appointed: October 1990

Star Performers

Frode Grodas
Position: goalkeeper
Club: Chelsea (England)
Born: October 24, 1964

Henning Berg
Position: defender
Club: Manchester United (England)
Born: September 1, 1969

Kjetil Rekdal
Position: midfield
Club: Hertha Berlin (Germany)
Born: November 6, 1968

Lars Bohinen
Position: midfield
Club: Blackburn Rovers (England)
Born: September 8, 1969

Ole Gunnar Solskjaer
Position: forward
Club: Manchester United (England)
Born: February 26, 1973

Stale Solbakken
Position: midfield
Club: Wimbledon (England)
Born: February 27, 1968

The Road to the Finals

Norway 5–0 Azerbaijan
Norway 3–0 Hungary
Switzerland 0–1 Norway
Norway 1–1 Finland
Hungary 1–1 Norway
Finland 0–4 Norway
Azerbaijan 0–1 Norway
Norway 5–0 Switzerland

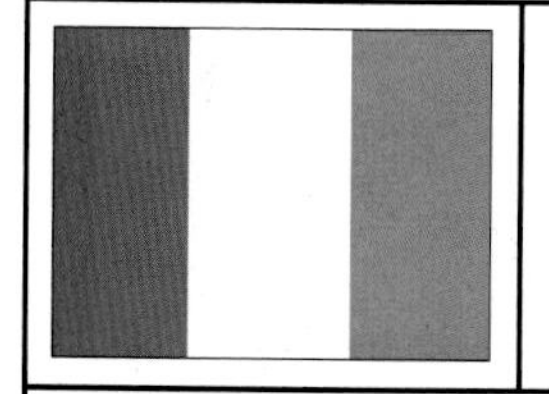

ITALY

Almost too good to be true

Group B

Italy's players are among the most talented and disciplined in the world, their coaches among the most tactically sophisticated, their fans among the most passionate.

Italian clubs have won seven World Club Cups, nine European Champions Cups, six European Cup-Winners Cups, eight UEFA Cups and six European Supercups.

But strength in depth has been demonstrated most clearly in the World Cup: Italy were the first nation in Europe to host the finals and the first in Europe to win three times – 1934, 1938 and 1982.

The national team, however, took a back seat as big clubs invested lavishly in foreign stars. The Azzurri paid a heavy penalty: they were beaten in the first round of the finals in 1954 and failed to even qualify in 1958. In Chile in 1962 Italy fell in a first-round punch-up with their hosts; in 1966 they were eliminated by North Korea.

As European Championship hosts in 1968, Italy defeated Yugoslavia in the Final only after a replay. The nucleus of that team were runners-up to a magnificent Brazil in the World Cup in Mexico two years later, followed by victory in Spain in 1982.

Enzo Bearzot's men were past their best in Mexico in 1986 and his successor, Azeglio Vicini, was short on luck when Italy were hosts again in 1990. They went out to Argentina in a semi-final penalty shoot-out.

More shoot-out pain followed four years later when Italy, having reached the Final, lost on penalties to Brazil in Pasadena. Coach Arrigo Sacchi was replaced by Cesare Maldini after a disappointing couple of years. Maldini's reign began in earnest with a 1–0 victory at Wembley in February 1997, but Italy dropped points in 0–0 draws against Poland and Georgia and – most devastatingly – at home to England.

Italy finished the group unbeaten with only one goal against, but second best. Russia awaited them in the play-offs. In the Moscow snow Italy regained their self-respect and forced a 1–1 draw; back home, Pierluigi Casiraghi hit the only goal.

Ironically, considering their qualifying problems, Italy went to France as one of the top seeds. But Maldini was not fooled, saying: " We need to improve a lot. We must be ready for anything."

The nucleus of the team is there. Angelo Peruzzi is an experienced, trophy-winning goalkeeper. Maldini's son Paolo and Alessandro Costacurta provide the old heads in defence. Demitri Albertini, Roberto Di Matteo and Dino Baggio provide a strong midfield platform. This leaves just the attack to sort out, with the options of Christian Vieri, Casiraghi and Fabrizio Ravanelli to provide the force, and Allesandro Del Piero and Gianfranco Zola the creative link.

Italy braved the Russian snow before winning the second play-off leg at home

World Cup Record

1930	did not enter	**1970**	runners up
1934	champions	**1974**	finals 1st round
1938	champions	**1978**	4th place
1950	finals 1st round	**1982**	champions
1954	finals 1st round	**1986**	finals 2nd round
1958	failed to qualify	**1990**	3rd place
1962	finals 1st round	**1994**	runners up
1966	finals 1st round		

The Coach

Cesare Maldini
Career: played for Milan; coached Milan, Foggia, Ternana, Parma, Italy's under-21 and Olympic teams.
Born: February 5, 1932
Appointed: January 1997

Star Performers

Paolo Maldini
Position: defender
Club: Milan
Born: June 26, 1968

Alessandro Costacurta
Position: central defender
Club: Milan
Born: April 24, 1966

Dino Baggio
Position: midfield
Club: Parma
Born: July 24, 1971

Alessandro Del Piero
Position: forward
Club: Juventus
Born: November 9, 1974

Christian Vieri
Position: striker
Club: Atletico Madrid (Spain)
Born: July 12, 1973

Gianfranco Zola
Position: forward
Club: Chelsea (England)
Born: July 5, 1966

The Road to the Finals

Moldova 1–3 Italy
Italy 1–0 Georgia
England 0–1 Italy
Italy 3–0 Moldova
Poland 0–0 Italy
Italy 3–0 Poland
Georgia 0–0 Italy
Italy 0–0 England
Russia 1–1 Italy*
Italy 1–0 Russia*

*Play-offs

CHILE

A passion for the game

Group B

All the legendary passion which pervades South American football was in evidence when Chile clinched South America's last qualifying place – reaching the finals for the first time in 16 years – by defeating hapless Bolivia 3–0 in Santiago last November.

Chile are superb at home but have yet to find the same confidence when they travel

Victory against neighbours Boliva sparked delirious celebrations throughout the country. Chile had to win because failure would have let in Peru or even Ecuador. In the end it all came down to goal difference. Chile took 25 points, scored 32 goals and conceded 18 (plus 14); Peru scored 19 and conceded 20 (minus one).

A 77,700 crowd jammed the Estadio Nacional to see first-half goals from Rodrigo Barrera and new superstar Marcelo Salas set Chile on their way. Substitute Juan Carreno rounded off the scoring five minutes from time to make it a comfortable 3–0 victory.

Qualification was a welcome prize after 12 troubled years in the World Cup wilderness. Chile is one of the oldest football strongholds in South America, the British football and linguistic tradition surviving in club names such as Wanderers, Green Cross, Everton, Rangers and the evocative Santiago Morning.

The federation was founded in 1895 but professionalism did not take root until after the creation of the Colo Colo club in 1925. They are the only Chilean side to have won a major prize, the Libertadores Cup in 1991.

Third as hosts

Chile went to the first World Cup in 1930, beat Mexico 3–0 and France 1–0, yet failed to progress beyond the first round. They did not put together another two-match winning sequence at the finals until they were hosts in 1962 – and finished a best-ever third.

The country had been ravaged by earthquakes, but federation president Carlos Dittborn told a worried FIFA: "We must have the World Cup because we have nothing else." Dittborn died shortly before the finals but his words were emblazoned across the scoreboards at the stadia.

Chile did not return to the finals until 1974, then failed to win a match, a sad tale repeated in 1982. They did not qualify for 1986 and missed out in 1990 after the team walked off during a qualifying tie against Brazil, claiming that goalkeeper Roberto Rojas had been hit by a firecracker. FIFA ruled that he had feigned his injury, and barred Chile from competing in 1994. With that ban in mind, captain and leading goalscorer Ivan Zamorano has warned: "An entire generation of Chilean players was denied the chance to go to the World Cup. We have a lot to prove."

World Cup Record

1930	finals 1st rnd	**1970**	did not qualify
1934	withdrew	**1974**	finals 1st rnd
1938	did not enter	**1978**	did not qualify
1950	finals 1st rnd	**1982**	finals 1st rnd
1954	did not qualify	**1986**	did not qualify
1958	did not qualify	**1990**	did not qualify
1962	third place	**1994**	suspended
1966	did not qualify		

The Coach

Nelson Acosta
Career: played in Uruguay for Huracan Buce and Penarol, then in Chile with Everton, O'Higgins and Fernandez Vial; coached Fernandez Vial, O'Higgins, Cruz Azul (Mexico) and Union Espanola.
Born: June 12, 1944 (in Uruguay)
Appointed: June 1996

Star Performers

Nelson Tapia
Position: goalkeeper
Club: Universidad Catolica
Born: September 22, 1966

Ivan Zamorano
Position: striker
Club: Internazionale (Italy)
Born: January 18, 1967

Ronald Fuentes
Position: central defender
Club: Universidad de Chile
Born: June 22, 1969

Marcelo Salas
Position: striker
Club: River Plate (Argentina)
Born: December 24, 1974

Luis Musrri
Position: midfield
Club: Universidad de Chile
Born: December 24, 1969

The Road to the Finals

Venezuela 1–1 Chile	Chile 6–0 Venezuela
Chile 4–1 Ecuador	Ecuador 1–1 Chile
Colombia 4–1 Chile	Chile 4–1 Colombia
Paraguay 2–1 Chile	Chile 2–1 Paraguay
Chile 1–0 Uruguay	Uruguay 1–0 Chile
Argentina 1–1 Chile	Chile 1–2 Argentina
Peru 2–1 Chile	Chile 4–0 Peru
Bolivia 1–1 Chile	Chile 3–0 Bolivia

CAMEROON

Saldanha's vision still in sight

Group B

Back in the 1970s the veteran Brazilian commentator and coach, Joao Saldanha, predicted that a Black African nation would win the World Cup before the end of the century. So far, Cameroon have gone closest to bringing Saldanha's vision to life.

Nobody will forget the excitement and drama they brought to the 1990 finals. They defeated holders Argentina by 1–0 in the Opening Match and went further than any other African nation by reaching the quarter-finals and leading England 2–1 before falling to two late penalties.

But Cameroon's success was not a one-off. Top clubs Canon and Tonnerre of Yaounde have proved among the most successful in the African club competitions, and Cameroon, after reaching the World Cup finals for the first time in 1982 and leaving Spain unbeaten at the end of the first round, were African champions in 1988.

Two of their 1990 World Cup veteran heroes, goalkeeper Thomas Nkono and spearhead Roger Milla, are among players to have been African Footballer of the Year, Milla being the first to win twice. Both were selected to play for a World XI against Brazil in late 1990.

Four years later Cameroon were back at the World Cup finals in the United States. It was a humbling experience. Internal problems hampered their preparation and the squad were perhaps too willing to believe their own over-ambitious publicity.

Now Cameroon are back, and they have even snatched one player away from the World Cup hosts. Striker Joseph-Desire Job of Lyon was about to play for France in the European Under-21 championship when Cameroon officials realised that he was eligible for them through parentage. He needed very little persuading to switch allegiance.

Tight to the finish

Qualifying for the World Cup was not easy. Cameroon were grouped with Angola, Zimbabwe and Togo. They beat Togo 4–2 but lost ground when held goalless at home by Angola. Narrow wins at home to Zimbabwe and Togo were followed by a 1–1 draw in Angola and left the qualifying issue wide open on the last day.

Cameroon flew to Zimbabwe with 11 points while Angola, also away, were on 10 points as they faced Togo. Cameroon had to win to be sure of qualifying – and two goals from Japan-based Patrick Mboma achieved it. Angola managed only a 1–1 draw in Togo.

Belgian coach Henri Depireux guided Cameroon to the finals but left immediately afterwards and was succeeded by former international Jean Manga Onguene. Cameroon used 41 players last year in all games but the nucleus is likely to be built around veteran goalkeeper Jacques Songo'o, right-back Rigobert Song, midfielder Marc-Viven Foe and strikers Job and Mboma.

Their challenge: to make Saldanha's dream come true.

Cameroon will be in France for Africa's last chance to win a World Cup this century

World Cup Record

1930	did not enter	**1970**	did not enter
1934	did not enter	**1974**	failed to qualify
1938	did not enter	**1978**	failed to qualify
1950	did not enter	**1982**	finals 1st round
1954	did not enter	**1986**	failed to qualify
1958	did not enter	**1990**	quarter-finals
1962	did not enter	**1994**	finals first round
1966	did not enter		

The Coach

Jean Manga Onguene
Career: played for Canon Yaoundé; coached the Cameroon junior teams and was assistant coach at the 1990 and 1994 World Cup finals.
Born: March 17, 1947
Appointed: July 1997

Star Performers

Jacques Songo'o
Position: goalkeeper
Club: La Coruña (Spain)
Born: March 17, 1964

Rigobert Song
Position: right-back
Club: Metz (France)
Born: July 1, 1976

Marc-Vivien Foe
Position: midfield
Club: Lens (France)
Born: May 1, 1975

Patrick Mboma
Position: forward
Club: Gamba Osaka (Japan)
Born: November 15, 1970

Joseph-Desire Job
Position: forward
Club: Lyon (France)
Born: December 1, 1977

The Road to the Finals

Togo 2–4 Cameroon	Cameroon 2–0 Togo
Cameroon 0–0 Angola	Angola 1–1 Cameroon
Cameroon 1–0 Zimbabwe	Zimbabwe 1–2 Cameroon

AUSTRIA

Prohaska heads a major revival

Group B

Austrian football is picking up. Champions Rapid Vienna were runners-up in the 1995–96 Cup-winners Cup and competed bravely against Juventus and Manchester United in the following season's UEFA Champions League.

Austria were almost certain to qualify even before their final qualifying game against Belarus

Having won away to the Irish Republic and apparently seized the initiative for Euro 96, Austria then lost away to Latvia and Northern Ireland to snatch failure from the jaws of qualification. Now they are back on the biggest stage of all after holding their nerve impressively to finish ahead of Scotland in European qualifying group four.

A 0–0 draw at home to Scotland in August 1996 was not the best start to the qualifying campaign. The Austrian media considered it two points dropped and that the psychological advantage had been handed not only to the Scots but to Sweden, group favourites.

In such circumstances, a journey to Stockholm next time out was the most awkward prospect possible. But midfielder Andy Herzog snatched a breakaway goal after 11 minutes and Austria – with goalkeeper Michael Konsel in superb form – hung on for a victory which turned the group on its head.

A month later Herzog scored again to grab a 2–1 win over Latvia, and Austria at last began to believe in themselves. A 2–0 defeat in Scotland was only a temporary setback.

Nine men hang on

The decisive match was staged in a packed Ernst-Happel stadium (formerly Prater) on September 6, against Sweden. Again Herzog scored the only goal for a victory, despite finishing with nine men after the expulsions of Konsel and Anton Pfeffer.

Manager and former midfield star Prohaska will take a settled, experienced team to France. Sweeper Wolfgang Feiersinger and full-back Peter Schottel have gained great European club experience with Borussia Dortmund and Rapid Vienna respectively. Up front Toni Polster, though now 34, has been one of the most consistent marksmen in European football over the past 15 years.

A doubt hangs over Herzog, ruled out for several months by a foot injury. But, as Prohaska says: "We are not a one-man team. I wouldn't want it that way."

World Cup Record

1930	did not enter	**1966**	did not qualify
1934	fourth place	**1970**	did not qualify
1938	qualified for finals, withdrew	**1974**	did not qualify
		1978	finals 2nd rnd
1950	did not qualify	**1982**	finals 2nd rnd
1954	third place	**1986**	did not qualify
1958	finals 1st rnd	**1990**	finals 1st rnd
1962	did not enter	**1994**	did not qualify

The Coach

Herbert Prohaska
Career: played for FK Austria, Internazionale (Italy), Roma (Italy); coached FK Austria and the national under-21s.
Born: August 8, 1955
Appointed: July 1994

Star Performers

Michael Konsel
Position: goalkeeper
Club: Roma (Italy)
Born: March 6, 1962

Wolfgang Feiersinger
Position: sweeper /midfield
Club: Borussia Dortmund (Germany)
Born: January 30, 1965

Andy Herzog
Position: midfield
Club: Werder Bremen (Germany)
Born: Sept 10, 1968

Dietmar "Didi" Kuehbauer
Position: midfield
Club: Real Sociedad (Spain)
Born: April 4, 1971

Toni Polster
Position: centre-forward
Club: Köln (Germany)
Born: March 10, 1964

The Road to the Finals

Austria 0–0 Scotland
Sweden 0–1 Austria
Austria 2–0 Latvia
Scotland 2–0 Austria
Austria 2–0 Estonia
Latvia 1–3 Austria
Estonia 0–3 Austria
Austria 1–0 Sweden
Belarus 0–1 Austria
Austria 4–0 Belarus

Austrian players celebrate their 4–0 victory over Belarus which clinched first place in their qualifying group

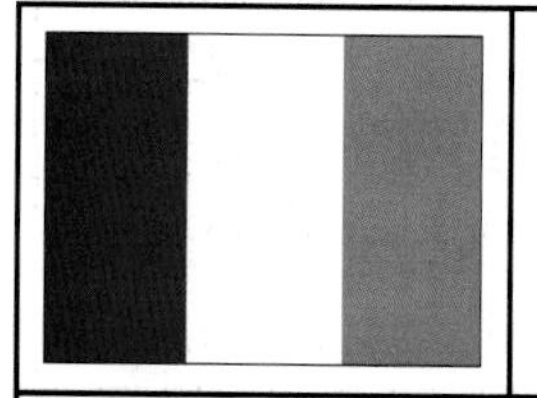

FRANCE

Hosts need to climb a mountain

Group C

France will be hosting the World Cup for the second time – and hoping to improve on 1938, when they were knocked out in the quarter-finals by holders Italy.

France hope to become the first hosts to win the World Cup for 20 years

After football legend Michel Platini relinquished the post of national manager after the 1992 European Championship, Aime Jacquet carries the hopes of the nation. The squad is packed with talent – but divining the correct combination has not proved the easiest of tasks.

The experience and intelligence of Didier Deschamps, allied to the attacking invention of Zinedine Zidane, were demonstrated to international effect when Juventus strode through to the 1997 Champions League Final. Alongside or behind them is Marcel Desailly, a European club champion with both Marseille and Milan. On the right is his new Milan colleague, Ibrahim Ba, with the Basque Bixente Lizarazu, on the left, always eager to roam up in support of his forwards.

Between midfield and attack is Youri Djorkaeff, whose intelligent wanderings make him almost impossible to tie down.

But here is a problem for Jacquet: almost all his key players are with clubs outside of France – and not all of them are guaranteed regular first-team football.

Hosts under pressure

Such is the dilemma facing Christophe Dugarry, one of the few "real" centre-forwards the French game has produced. After starring in Bordeaux's run to the 1996 UEFA Cup Final he has been merely a reserve de luxe at first Milan and then Barcelona.

The evidence of the two-week Tournoi de France last summer was not encouraging for the hosts. For all their technical excellence, France failed to win any of their three games and only a 2–2 draw with weakened, tiring Italy in the last saved them from bottom place. As Jacquet said: "Right now, the World Cup looks like a huge mountain to climb."

"Fatigue played a significant part in our results," he said. "We conceded an 85th-minute goal against England and a last-minute equaliser to Italy. But when it comes to the World Cup finals, we will have more time to prepare – we will be refreshed."

The entire French nation hopes Jacquet is proved right.

World Cup Record

1930	finals 1st round	**1970**	did not qualify
1934	finals 1st rnd	**1974**	did not qualify
1938	quarter-finals	**1978**	finals 1st rnd
1950	did not qualify	**1982**	fourth place
1954	finals 1st rnd	**1986**	third place
1958	third place	**1990**	did not qualify
1962	did not qualify	**1994**	did not qualify
1966	finals 1st rnd		

The Coach

Aime Jacquet
Career: played for Saint-Etienne, Lyon; coached Lyon, Bordeaux, Montpellier and Nancy and then became assistant to national coach Gerard Houllier.
Born: November 27, 1941
Appointed: December 1993

Star Performers

Laurent Blanc
Position: sweeper
Club: Marseille
Born: November 19, 1965

Zinedine Zidane
Position: midfield
Club: Juventus (Italy)
Born: June 23, 1972

Marcel Desailly
Position: midfield/ centre-back
Club: Milan (Italy)
Born: September 7, 1968

Youri Djorkaeff
Position: midfield/ forward
Club: Internazionale (Italy)
Born: March 9, 1968

Didier Deschamps
Position: midfielder
Club: Juventus (Italy)
Born: October 15, 1968

Marcel Desailly can play either in defence or midfield

SOUTH AFRICA

The Boys are right to be proud

Group C

South Africa will be the proudest nation in France, only six years since they returned to international football after 30 years in sporting isolation.

South Africa hope a good World Cup will enhance their chances of being hosts in 2006

World Cup Record

This is South Africa's first visit to the World Cup Finals

The Coach

Philippe Troussier
Career: coached Kaizer Chiefs (South Africa), Ivory Coast, Nigeria and Burkina Faso.

Born: March 21, 1955
Appointed: January 1998

Star Performers

Mark Fish
Position: central defender
Club: Bolton Wanderers (England)
Born: March 14, 1974

Lucas Radebe
Position: central defender
Club: Leeds United (England)
Born: April 2, 1969

Eric Tinkler
Position: midfield
Club: Barnsley (England)
Born: July 20, 1970

Shaun Bartlett
Position: striker
Club: New York-New Jersey MetroStars (United States)
Born: October 31, 1972

Phil Masinga
Position: forward
Club: Bari (Italy)
Born: June 28, 1969

The Road to the Finals

South Africa 1–0 Zaire*
Zambia 0–0 South Africa
Congo 2–0 South Africa
Zaire* 1–2 South Africa
South Africa 3–0 Zambia
South Africa 1–0 Congo

*Zaire now Congo DR

Soccer was always the No. 1 sport in South Africa and the first considered to have been organised on multi-ethnic lines. When South Africa returned to the FIFA fold in 1992 they initially struggled, but within four years had a leading role in the African game. First they stepped in at short notice to host the 1996 African Nations Cup finals – and went on to win the tournament, for the first time too.

That triumph, along with home draws against Argentina and Germany, lifted Bafana Bafana ("The Boys") into the top 20 in FIFA's monthly rankings. Now the Republic is considering bidding to become the first African World Cup host, in 2006.

Coach Clive Barker, a South African who played for Durban United, took over in 1994 after his country had had four coaches in quick succession. He succeeded where the others failed, melding a team out of talented individuals. More than half his squad now play in Europe or America, such as English-based defenders Mark Fish and Lucas Radebe and midfielder Eric Tinkler, Spain-based Steve Motaung and US-based striker Shaun Bartlett. Barker kept faith in a tried and tested squad who lost only three times in two dozen games up to the start of the World Cup qualifying campaign. But progress was not as smooth as he would have liked.

Masinga's winner

The African qualifying competition was a mixed format, starting with a direct knock-out round and then moving into mini-leagues with the three winners going to the finals. After beating Malawi in the first round, Barker's team had a 1–0 home win over Zaire, then drew 0–0 away to a Zambian team fired with enormous passion for the World Cup because of the air crash which wiped out most of their team and wrecked their bid to reach the finals in 1994.

A 2–0 defeat away to Congo was a minor hitch, and after two more victories over Zaire and Zambia, South Africa defeated Congo 1–0 to claim their tickets to the finals.

A 90,000 crowd turned out in Johannesburg to celebrate the occasion, and a 14th-minute goal from Phil Masinga decided match, group and qualification. Masinga was South Africa's top scorer in the qualifying rounds with four goals and Radebe, who had joined Leeds at the same time as Masinga, was oustanding in defence. Barker, asked about South Africa's ambitions, admitted that he didn't expect to win the World Cup – but he was confident his team might be the best outside bet.

SAUDI ARABIA

On the march at last

Group C

Saudi Arabia return to the World Cup finals for the second successive time with none of their opponents in any doubt that, after years of expectation, soccer is on the march in the Gulf states.

The Saudi Arabians have impressed many on their way to the finals of France 98

Over the past two decades or more, the Saudis have pumped millions of dollars into football, but had to wait until 1994 before the dividends began to flow back. Then, on their first appearance in the World Cup finals, they not only reached the second round from a group which included Holland and Belgium, but contributed one of the greatest individual goals in World Cup history.

The scorer, Sayeed Al-Owairan, may well be in France to bring his inspirational magic and vital experience to bear on another Saudi effort.

The Saudi Arabian national football association was founded in 1959 and the national team became a regular competitor in regional championships in the mid-1970s.

In 1975 the federation hired Ferenc Puskas, the legendary Hungarian, to set up a national team programme. The following year they entered the World Cup for the first time, only to be eliminated in the second round of the Asian qualifying section.

That failure was a spur to Saudi ambition. Clubs were granted permission for foreign coaches and English and then Brazilian managers brought their influence to bear. The Brazilian style proved more successful, with the players attracted to the more technical and individualistic method.

Money was also invested in infrastructure, notably the King Fahad stadium in Riyadh. Clubs such as Al Ahly, Al Hilal and Al Nasr have enjoyed success in the Asian club competitions. The first success for the Saudis at national team level was in 1989, when their teenagers won the World Junior (under-17) Championship in Scotland.

Success in 1994

Five years later several of those players had graduated to the senior side who reached USA '94. They lost 2–1 to Holland – after leading 1–0 – and defeated Morocco and Belgium. In the second round they lost honourably to Sweden.

The Saudis underlined their improvement by maintaining their regional domination. In 1996 they reached the Asian Cup Final for the fourth successive time and won for the third.

To qualify for France '98, the Saudis beat Iran 1–0 to reach the last qualifying match against Qatar, and then the same result gave them their first away victory and a place in the finals. Brazilian coach Carlos Alberto Parreira will be in charge and will be appearing in his fourth successive finals, each time with a different team.

World Cup Record

1930	did not enter	**1970**	did not enter
1934	did not enter	**1974**	did not enter
1938	did not enter	**1978**	did not qualify
1950	did not enter	**1982**	did not qualify
1954	did not enter	**1986**	did not qualify
1958	did not enter	**1990**	did not qualify
1962	did not enter	**1994**	finals 2nd rnd
1966	did not enter		

The Coach

Carlos Alberto Parreira
Career: did not play as a senior professional; coached Kuwait, United Arab Emirates and Brazil at the World Cup finals as well as Fenerbahce (Turkey) and New Jersey-New York Metrostars (USA).
Born: March 25, 1943
Appointed: Appointed: December 1997

Star Performers

Mohammed Al-Daeyea
Position: goalkeeper
Club: Al-Tae
Born: August 2, 1972

Sami Al-Jaber
Position: forward
Club: Al-Hilal
Born: December 11, 1972

Ahmed Al-Madani
Position: defender
Club: Al-Ittihad
Born: January 6, 1970

Sayeed Al-Owairan
Position: forward
Club: Al-Shabab
Born: August 19, 1967

Khalid Al-Muwalid
Position: midfield
Club: Al-Ahli
Born: November 23, 1971

The Road to the Finals

Saudi Arabia 2–1 Kuwait	Kuwait 2–1 Saudi Arabia
Iran 1–1 Saudi Arabia	Saudi Arabia 1–0 Iran
China 1–0 Saudi Arabia	Saudi Arabia 0–0 China
Saudi Arabia 1–0 Qatar	Qatar 0–1 Saudi Arabia

DENMARK

Bo and Co. have a go

Group C

Denmark, surprisingly, have attended the finals on only one previous occasion – in 1986 – when they reached the second round in Mexico before crashing to a spectacular 5–1 defeat by Spain.

That record is all the more surprising considering the high profile that Danish football has achieved ever since the early 1980s, when they reached the semi-finals of the European Championship. But the last qualifying group match then proved a step too far: Romania for 1990 and then Spain for 1994 both edged out the Danes when they were 90 minutes from the finals.

Swedish-born boss Bo Johansson – appointed in the summer of 1996 – had a good start with a 1–0 friendly victory in his native land with his first game. There also was a new captain in goalkeeper Peter Schmeichel and a 4–4–2 formation instead of the 3–5–2 which Richard Moller Nielsen had employed. Then came a battling 2–0 away win over Slovenia in Denmark's opening World Cup qualifier.

Slovenia and Bosnia offered only lightweight opposition and Greece had slipped back since reaching the 1994 finals, so it all came down to a straight battle against Croatia – and a welcome chance of instant revenge for a 3–0 defeat in Euro 96. Michael Laudrup snatched an equaliser eight minutes from time in the first match and when Denmark won the return 3–1 – Laudrup again on the scoresheet – they were home and dry.

Sound if not spectacular

Johansson has made significant changes, not only in tactics but also in selection. Players and media quickly took to him, after initial surprise at the appointment of a man respected but not exactly the household name some critics had been expecting. He introduced some novel ideas – such as encouraging players to hug each other in training to improve team spirit – and charmed the media.

Denmark reached the European Championship finals in 1984, under the leadership of former German international Sepp Piontek. This was an exciting new team built around exiled professionals and nicknamed "Danish Dynamite" by the fans.

Denmark's 3–1 victory over Croatia in September 1997 booked their place in France

World Cup Record

1930	did not enter	**1970**	did not qualify
1934	did not enter	**1974**	did not qualify
1938	did not enter	**1978**	did not qualify
1950	did not enter	**1982**	did not qualify
1954	did not enter	**1986**	finals 2nd round
1958	failed to qualify	**1990**	failed to qualify
1962	did not enter	**1994**	failed to qualify
1966	did not qualify		

The Coach

Bo Johansson
Career: born in Sweden; played for Kalmar; coached Kalmar, Lindsals, Oster Vaxjo, Djerv (Norway), Panionios (Greece), the Iceland national team, Silkeborg (Denmark) and HJK Helsinki (Finland).
Born: November 28, 1942
Appointed: July 1996

Star Performers

Peter Schmeichel
Position: goalkeeper
Club: Manchester United (England)
Born: November 18, 1963

Jes Hogh
Position: central defender
Club: Fenerbahce (Turkey)
Born: May 7, 1966

Jan Heintze
Position: leftback
Club: Bayer Leverkusen (Germany)
Born: August 17, 1963

Michael Laudrup
Position: midfield
Club: Ajax (Holland)
Born: June 15, 1964

Brian Laudrup
Position: forward
Club: Rangers (Scotland)
Born: September 22, 1969

The Road to the Finals

Slovenia 0–2 Denmark	Denmark 2–0 Bosnia
Denmark 2–1 Greece	Bosnia 3–0 Denmark
Croatia 1–1 Denmark	Denmark 3–1 Croatia
Denmark 4–0 Slovenia	Greece 0–0 Denmark

They reached the second round of the 1986 World Cup, the first round of the 1988 European Championship – and then carried off the European title in 1992.

The manner of that triumph is part of footballing legend. Denmark, called up late when Yugoslavia were excluded because of their civil war, went to beat reigning world champions Germany by 2–0 in the Final.

As former captain Morten Olsen put it: "Our secret is that we are friends. And you run harder and work harder for your friends than you do for workmates."

SPAIN

At last, dreams have come true

Group D

Javier Clemente is a manager who made dreams come true for Spain. Most managers boast that they will recreate the tight, claustrophobic atmosphere of a club side: very few achieve it. Clemente is the exception.

His personal success has been reflected in Spain's apparently permanent presence among the world's leading football nations.

Spain's national team used to be poor relations in their own country. The fans cared much more about the triumphs of Real Madrid, Barcelona and Atletico Madrid – club teams packed full of exotic foreign stars – in the three European club competitions. The national side appeared to be some sort of "fourth team" by comparison.

Clemente, however, has changed all that, and is now firmly in the driving seat. He is a tough, resilient Basque, and has built the most solid foundations. Of the 11 starters plus two substitutes beaten by Italy at USA '94, only two failed to survive through to Spain's Euro 96 squad and unlucky defeat by England, and no fewer than eight were in both those quarter-finals.

The backbone of Clemente's team has been formed by veteran Basque goalkeeper Andoni Zubizarreta – who holds Spain's record for international appearances, well over 100 – Miguel Angel Nadal, Fernando Hierro, Luis Enrique and Jose Luis Caminero.

Zubizarreta, the world's most expensive goalkeeper at £1.2 million when he left Bilbao for Barcelona in 1986, has long been Clemente's trusty captain: "I leave it until as late as possible to tell my players the team – with the exception of Zubi. I tell him the night before."

Loyal to his players

Club form is immaterial to Clemente. Once he has bonded a player into the national squad then that player stays, whether first choice for his club or reserve. For example, Santiago Canizares was Zubizarreta's regular No. 2 while a season-long reserve at Real Madrid.

Clemente has not escaped criticism that he has remained too loyal too long to some older players – especially when he went to Euro 96 without emerging superstarlets Raul from Real Madrid and Ivan de la Pena from Barcelona. Clemente reasoned that inexperience would weigh too heavy but he was not blind to their talent, as shown by the speed with which he then summoned them for the World Cup campaign.

World Cup Record

1930	did not enter	**1970**	did not qualify
1934	quarter-finals	**1974**	did not qualify
1938	did not enter	**1978**	finals 1st rnd
1950	fourth place	**1982**	finals 2nd rnd
1954	did not qualify	**1986**	quarter-finals
1958	did not qualify	**1990**	finals 2nd rnd
1962	finals 1st rnd	**1994**	quarter-finals
1966	finals 1st rnd		

The Coach

Javier Clemente
Career: played for Athletic Bilbao; coached Bilbao, Espanol, Atletico Madrid, Espanyol
Born: March 12, 1950.
Appointed: July 1992

Star Performers

Andoni Zubizarreta
Position: goalkeeper
Club: Valencia
Born: October 23, 1961

Julen Guerrero
Position: midfielder
Club: Atletico Bilbao
Born: January 7, 1974

Miguel Angel Nadal
Position: central defender
Club: Barcelona
Born: July 28, 1966

Raul Gonzalez
Position: forward
Club: Real Madrid
Born: June 27, 1977

Fernando Hierro
Position: central defender
Club: Real Madrid
Born: March 23, 1968

Josep Guardiola
Position: forward
Club: Barcelona
Born: January 18, 1971

The Road to the Finals

Faroe Is 2–6 Spain
Czech Rep 0–0 Spain
Spain 4–1 Slovakia
Spain 2–0 Yugoslavia
Malta 0–3 Spain
Spain 4–0 Malta
Yugoslavia 1–1 Spain
Spain 1–0 Czech Rep
Slovakia 1–2 Spain
Spain 3–1 Faroe Is

Spain line up before beating the Faroe Islands 3–1 to clinch their berth in France

Spain were one of the first European qualifiers for France '98. They thrashed the Faroe Islands 6–2 in their first game, a goalless draw in the Czech Republic was followed by clear-cut wins over Slovakia and Yugoslavia, and seven goals were claimed in two victories over Malta. Then Hierro struck vital goals to earn a 1–1 draw in Yugoslavia and a 1–0 home win over the Czechs.

On October 11, a 3–1 home win against the Faroes confirmed Spain's group victory. No fewer than six of that team had been quarter-final losers four years ago. Once more, loyalty had paid off for Clemente.

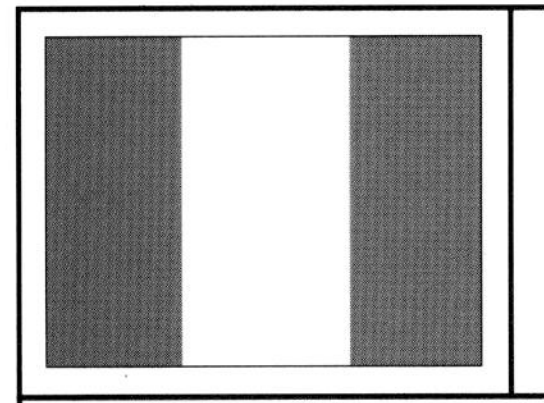

NIGERIA

Out to be Africa's best

Group D

The 1998 World Cup finals will be notable as the first for which an African nation will be considered among contenders – albeit outside contenders – to win the greatest prize in the game.

Nigeria's Olympic Games gold medal in 1996 makes them an outside bet in 1998

Nigeria are that nation, having been among the first to secure their qualifying place. Their status as Olympic champions and their record of a second-round place four years ago lifts them above the likes of Cameroon in the frame.

Nigeria have other credentials. They won the FIFA World Under-17 Cup in 1985 and 1993, won the African Nations Cup in 1994, and won the Olympic Games title last year.

Using a nucleus of players from USA '94, they scored sensational victories over Mexico (2–0), over favourites Brazil (4–3) and then Argentina (3–2) in the Final.

Cosmopolitan stars of the Olympic team who could well enhance their reputations in France include defender Taribo West (now with Internazionale), fullback Celestine Babayaro (Chelsea), Ajax winger Tijani Babangida, Betis flyer Finidi George, Fenerbahce midfielder Jay-Jay Okocha, Monaco's Victor Ikpeba and Inter's Nwankwo Kanu.

Nigeria had long been considered potentially the most powerful of the Black African nations. They had consistently impressed in world age-group tournaments, and that success is being recognized next year when Nigeria will host the World Youth Cup.

At France 98 Okocha will be one of the "wise old heads" – having marked his Nigeria senior debut with a brilliant goal against Ivory Coast in only his second international.

Great inspiration

Ahead of him in Nigeria's attack is Victor Ikpeba. Out on the wings Nigeria are likely to profit from the skills of George and former African Footballer of the Year Amunike. They will be needed to supply the bullets for Daniel Amokachi and Kanu to fire – and it is Kanu who will be the greatest inspiration of all.

Almost two years ago, after his transfer from Ajax to Inter, Kanu was diagnosed as having a congenital heart defect. He was told that, at 21, his football was over. But Inter scoured the world for top surgeons and Kanu has returned to action.

Nigeria qualified among the initial wave of hopefuls, last June. A 3–0 win at home to Kenya took them to the top of African qualifying Group One with a game in hand. Guinea beat them 1–0 then but it was too little, too late.

Michel Platini, joint president of the French World Cup organising committee, is thrilled by the prospect of seeing the Nigerians again. He says: "They will give the French public a great deal of enjoyment. It wouldn't surprise me if they went further than any African team have ever gone before."

World Cup Record

1930	did not enter	**1970**	did not qualify
1934	did not enter	**1974**	did not qualify
1938	did not enter	**1978**	did not qualify
1950	did not enter	**1982**	did not qualify
1954	did not enter	**1986**	did not qualify
1958	did not enter	**1990**	did not qualify
1962	did not enter	**1994**	finals 2nd rnd
1966	did not enter		

The Coach

Vellbor "Bora" Milutanovic
Career: coached UNAM (Mexico), Udinese (Italy), San Lorenzo (Argentina), UAG and Veracruz (both Mexico), Mexico, Costa Rica and United States.
Born: September 7, 1944
Appointed: January 1998

Star Performers

Taribo West
Position: Left-back
Club: Internazionale (Italy)
Born: March 26, 1974

Finidi George
Position: forward
Club: Real Betis (Spain)
Born: April 15, 1971

Celestine Babayaro
Position: defender
Club: Chelsea (England)
Born: August 29, 1978

Victor Ikpeba
Position: forward
Club: Monaco (France)
Born: June 12, 1973

Augustine "Jay Jay" Okocha
Position: midfield
Club: Fenerbahce (Turkey)
Born: August 14, 1973

Nwankwo Kanu
Position: forward
Club: Internazionale (Italy)
Born: August 1, 1976

The Road to the Finals

Nigeria 2–0 Burkina Faso	Burkina Faso 1–2 Nigeria
Kenya 1–1 Nigeria	Nigeria 3–0 Kenya
Nigeria 2–1 Guinea	Guinea 1–0 Nigeria

PARAGUAY

Plenty of cause for pride

Group D

Paraguay is home to the South American football confederation, CONMEBOL. But pride in that matter of football fact is by far overshadowed by fans' pride in the nation's football – and the manner in which they qualified for the 1998 World Cup finals.

In terms of South American hierarchy, Paraguay come some way down the list, but they have now qualified for the World Cup finals for the fifth time, they have former world club champions in Olimpia, and in goalkeeper Jose Luis Chilavert – 1996 South American Footballer of the Year – one of the game's great characters.

The bustling capital of Asuncion dominates football in Paraguay. The first league was created way back in 1906 and it now has more than 30 clubs – the strongest being Olimpia, winners of the Libertadores Cup in 1979 and 1990.

Paraguay appeared at the inaugural World Cup finals in Uruguay in 1930, losing 3–0 to the United States, beating Belgium 1–0, and then promptly disappeared from sight until the 1950s. They went out in the first round in both 1950 and 1958, not to return for another 28 years. That was in Mexico in 1986 when they also posted their best performance: they progressed to the second round, having gone undefeated through the group stage, before losing 3–0 to a Gary Lineker-inspired England.

'Keeper to the fore

The outstanding personality then was goalkeeper Roberto Fernandez. He has been succeeded by an even more remarkable character in Chilavert, a regular goal-scorer from free-kicks and penalties, but whose temper has brought him into confrontations with opponents, team-mates, journalists and even a government minister's bodyguards.

After opening the 1998 World Cup campaign with a defeat in Colombia, Paraguay went eight matches unbeaten. That run included a 1–1 draw with Argentina in Buenos Aires, when Chilavert scored from a free-kick – as he had boasted he would do.

None of Chilavert's team-mates comes near his charisma or attracts comparative attention. Catalino Rivarola, Celso Ayala and Carlos Gamarra are experienced defenders, Julio Enciso a promising midfielder and Richard Baez a quick-witted striker, but Chilavert makes all the difference.

Paraguay beat Colombia 2–1 last April to go top of their group. But Chilavert was sent off and banned for four matches. In his absence, Paraguay lost three times and slipped to third. On his return, however, they beat Bolivia 2–1 to qualify for France.

Coach Paulo Cesar Carpeggiani is a Brazilian whose World Cup experience dates back to his playing days in 1974. He's worked hard to change the Paraguayan style from one which depended too much on the long ball to a more close-passing variety. "We've got it right now," he says. "We have some outstanding individuals capable of causing surprises."

Paraguay's record of seven home wins in eight qualifiers guaranteed their place in France

World Cup Record

1930	finals 1st rnd	**1970**	did not qualify
1934	did not enter	**1974**	did not qualify
1938	did not enter	**1978**	did not qualify
1950	finals 1st rnd	**1982**	did not qualify
1954	did not qualify	**1986**	finals 2nd rnd
1958	finals 1st rnd	**1990**	did not qualify
1962	did not enter	**1994**	did not qualify
1966	did not qualify		

The Coach

Paulo Cesar Carpeggiani
Career: played in Brazil for Internacional Porte Alegre and Flamengo; coached Flamengo and Internacional in Brazil.
Born: February 7, 1949
Appointed: February 1996

Star Performers

Jose Luis Chilavert
Position: goalkeeper
Club: Velez Sarsfield (Argentina)
Born: January 27, 1965

Catalino Rivarola
Position: defender
Club: Gremio (Brazil)
Born: April 30, 1966

Carlos Gamarra
Position: defender
Club: Internacional (Brazil)
Born: February 17, 1971

Julio Enciso
Position: midfield
Club: Cerro Porteno
Born: August 5, 1974

Enrique Benitez
Position: forward
Club: Espanyol (Spain)
Born: December 29, 1972

The Road to the Finals

Colombia 1–0 Paraguay	Paraguay 2–1 Colombia
Uruguay 0–2 Paraguay	Paraguay 3–1 Uruguay
Argentina 1–1 Paraguay	Paraguay 1–2 Argentina
Paraguay 2–1 Chile	Chile 2–1 Paraguay
Paraguay 1–0 Ecuador	Ecuador 2–1 Paraguay
Bolivia 0–0 Paraguay	Paraguay 2–1 Bolivia
Venezuela 0–2 Paraguay	Paraguay 1–0 Venezuela
Paraguay 2–1 Peru	Peru 1–0 Paraguay

"We won't make the same mistakes"

Group D

Bulgaria revolutionised their football image with the remarkable campaign which took them to fourth place in the 1994 World Cup finals.

Bulgaria will have one of the most experienced squads in France

Now, suddenly, Bulgaria were among the most dangerous of opponents, a nation replete with stars such as forwards Hristo Stoichkov and Emil Kostadinov and midfielders Yordan Lechkov and Krasimir Balakov.

At USA '94 they knocked out reigning champions Germany in the quarter-finals – with a historic headed goal from balding midfielder Lechkov – before falling in the semi-finals to Italy and, in the third-place play-off, to Sweden.

Unfortunately, complacency set in. Bulgaria qualified for the finals of the 1996 European Championship – again beating the Germans along the way – but fell in the first round of the finals. National coach Hristo Bonev is determined they will not make the same mistake twice.

Smooth passage

Bulgaria qualified surprisingly easily for France, whereupon coach Bonev immediately made it clear that the mistakes of campaigns past would not be repeated. Bonev told his players: "When I was playing we thought that qualifying for the finals was enough. It wasn't. We had the talent to do better and we wasted it through a lack of ambition and application.

"We must iron out certain weaknesses and build a team which will do our country justice in the finals. Each player knows he will be replaced by the next generation one day, and it will not be an easy task as this generation has been the most successful so far."

Back in the fold

Bonev has not had an easy ride since taking over as national coach from Dimitar Penev after the Euro 96 disappointment. The federation was racked by internal conflicts and Stoichkov – greatest Bulgarian footballer of all time – boycotted the national team for over a year in protest at the men running the sport.

Ultimately, Bonev persuaded Stoichkov to make his peace, and their conversation could prove one of the most important steps down the World Cup road for Bulgaria. With their talent and experience, they will be worth watching.

World Cup Record

1930	did not enter	**1970**	finals 1st rnd
1934	did not qualify	**1974**	finals 1st rnd
1938	did not qualify	**1978**	did not qualify
1950	did not enter	**1982**	did not qualify
1954	did not qualify	**1986**	finals 2nd rnd
1958	did not enter	**1990**	did not qualify
1962	finals 1st rnd	**1994**	fourth place
1966	finals 1st rnd		

The Coach

Hristo Bonev
Career: played for Lokomotiv Plovdiv, CSKA Sofia and AEK Athens; coached Panathinaikos, Ionikos (both Greece) and Apoel (Cyprus).
Born: February 3, 1947
Appointed: August 1996

Star Performers

Trifon Ivanov
Position: centre-back
Club: Rapid Vienna (Austria)
Born: July 27, 1965

Krasimir Balakov
Position: midfielder
Club: Stuttgart, (Germany)
Born: April 28, 1966

Yordan Lechkov
Position: midfield
Club: Galatasaray (Turkey)
Born: July 19, 1967

Hristo Stoichkov
Position: forward
Club: Barcelona (Spain)
Born: February 8, 1966

Emil Kostadinov
Position: centre-forward
Club: Fenerbahce (Turkey)
Born: August 12, 1967

The Road to the Finals

Israel 2–1 Bulgaria	Bulgaria 4–0 Luxembourg
Luxembourg 1–2 Bulgaria	Bulgaria 1–0 Israel
Cyprus 1–3 Bulgaria	Bulgaria 1–0 Russia
Bulgaria 4–1 Cyprus	Russia 4–2 Bulgaria

Bulgaria celebrate qualification after beating Russia 1–0 in Sofia

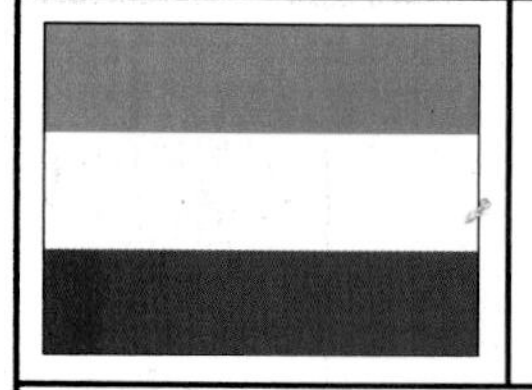

HOLLAND

A need to be united

Group E

Holland's rise to glory is one of football's fairytales. Until the 1974 World Cup, the Dutch had appeared in the finals only once, in 1938, when they went home after one match – beaten 3–0 by Czechoslovakia in Le Havre.

Holland's national side has failed to match the quality of her club sides

For the best part of the three succeeding decades Dutch football was considered among Europe's lesser lights. Then Feyenoord won the European Champions Cup in 1970, and Ajax Amsterdam did the same three years in a row.

They flourished with a revolutionary, free-wheeling style that became known as "total football" under coach Rinus Michels, who developed the tactic and found the players to express it in Arie Haan, Johan Neeskens, Ruud Krol, Wim Suurbier, Johnny Rep, Piet Keizer and, above all, the inspirational Johan Cruyff.

Holland finished runners-up to West Germany at the World Cup of 1974 and four years later, against Argentina, they again missed out in the final.

The Dutch became European champions in 1988 as a new galaxy of stars such as Ruud Gullit and Marco Van Basten shone brightly. But the arrogance which marked their football spilled over into problems off the pitch which undermined the squad.

Storm of dissent

Before the 1990 World Cup, player power forced the departure of coach Thijs Libregts; Holland went out in the second round. Four years later, controversy arose around Gullit's return and then almost instant departure from the team; Holland fell in the quarter-finals.

At least Guus Hiddink, who coached Holland to the quarter-finals of the 1996 European Championship, managed to ride a threatening storm of internal dissent.

Hiddink found room for PSV Eindhoven playmaker Wim Jonk alongside Ajax's Ronald De Boer in midfield; PSV's Jaap Stam alongside Ajax's Frank de Boer in central defence; Arsenal's Dennis Bergkamp supporting another Ajax exile in Milan's Patrick Kluivert up front.

Comfortable wins over Wales – twice – and in Belgium were followed by a surprise 1–0 defeat in Turkey. Significantly, perhaps, Bergkamp was unavailable for the tie because of his fear of flying.

In the return against Belgium, a goal from Stam gave Holland an interval lead, and Kluivert and Bergkamp struck later for a 3–1 win. A 0–0 home draw against Turkey was then enough to seal group victory.

Now Hiddink has in place a team of real potential built around Ajax and 1997 league champions PSV Eindhoven. And as for fears that the Dutch may somehow contrive to shoot themselves in the foot yet again, Hiddink says: "If there is a problem, then I will take care of it."

World Cup Record

1930 did not enter
1934 finals 1st rnd
1938 finals 1st rnd
1950 did not enter
1954 did not enter
1958 did not qualify
1962 did not qualify
1966 did not qualify
1970 did not qualify
1974 runners-up
1978 runners-up
1982 did not qualify
1986 did not qualify
1990 finals 2nd rnd
1994 quarter-finals

The Coach

Guus Hiddink
Career: played for Sport Varsseveld, De Graafschap, PSV Eindhoven and NEC Nijmegen and then in the United States with Washington Diplomats and San Jose Earthquakes; coached PSV Eindhoven, Fenerbahce and Valencia.
Born: November 8, 1946
Appointed: December 1994

Star Performers

Edwin Van der Saar
Position: goalkeeper
Club: Ajax Amsterdam
Born: October 29, 1970

Frank De Boer
Position: centre back
Club: Ajax Amsterdam
Born: May 15, 1970

Wim Jonk
Position: midfield
Club: PSV Eindhoven
Born: October 12, 1966

Clarence Seedorf
Position: midfield
Club: Real Madrid (Spain)
Born: April 1, 1976

Dennis Bergkamp
Position: forward
Club: Arsenal (England)
Born: May 10, 1969

The Road to the Finals

Wales 1–3 Holland
Holland 7–1 Wales
Belgium 0–3 Holland
Holland 4–0 San Marino
Turkey 1–0 Holland
San Marino 0–6 Holland
Holland 3–1 Belgium
Holland 0–0 Turkey

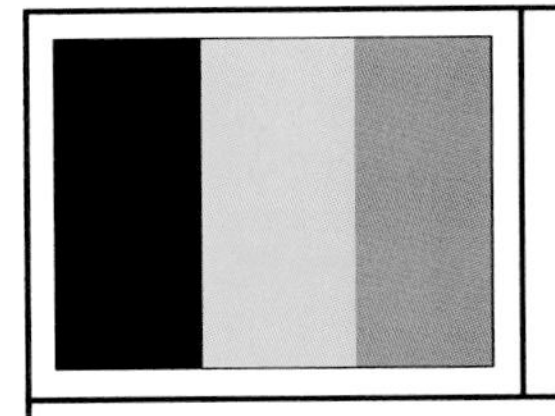

BELGIUM

The awkward neighbours

Group E

Belgium are assured of their place at the finals of the 2000 European Championship thanks to their status as joint hosts with Holland. Reaching the more immediate World Cup finals – their fifth sucessive appearance – threatened to be beyond them.

Opening wins in the qualification tournament at home to Turkey and away to San Marino were rendered almost meaningless after Belgium crashed 3–0 at home to Holland. That infuriated fans, depressed players and cost coach Wilfred Van Moer his job.

Over Christmas 1996 the federation decided to entrust the rescue operation to former international Georges Leekens. Prising him away from Excelsior Mouscron proved controversial, but a victory in Turkey meant that, even though their fiercest rivals Holland had another comfortable win, Belgium's defeat of Wales in the final match would guarantee a Playoff place.

Two late Welsh goals gave Belgium a fright, but their three earlier ones ensured a play-off berth as group runners-up. In Dublin, the Republic of Ireland were held 1–1, thanks to Luc Nilis' fine goal, and he scored the decisive second goal late in the game in Brussels, as Belgium beat the Republic in the second leg 2–1, to book their place in France.

Belgium will now be awkward opponents, if they play to the standard which saw them finish fourth in the 1986 World Cup and runners-up in the 1980 European Championship. The star of the era was midfielder Jan Ceulemans, and he has been succeeded by Enzo Scifo, who will be appearing in his fourth finals.

Scifo was eligible to play for both Italy and Belgium but he has always been more comfortable away from the oppressive spotlight of Italian football and after two unsuccesful spells in Serie A, he has returned to the club where he began his career, Anderlecht. The Brussels club are Belgium's most successful, having won two European competitions.

Although one of the few countries to appear in all the World Cup finals before World War II, Belgium did not win a game in the finals until their fifth appearance, in 1970. However, since 1982, the Belgians have been one of the most consistent teams, reaching at least the second round in the last four tournaments. Indeed, Belgium join Brazil, Argentina, Germany, Italy and Spain, as the only nations to have played in all of the last five finals.

As well as Scifo, Belgium will look to strikers Nilis and Oliveira – who could have played for Uruguay instead – to provide the goals to continue their proud recent record.

Following this 3–0 home defeat by Holland, Belgium appointed Georges Leekens coach

World Cup Record

1930 finals 1st round
1934 finals 1st round
1938 finals 1st round
1950 did not enter
1954 finals 1st round
1958 did not qualify
1962 did not qualify
1966 did not qualify
1970 finals 1st round
1974 did not qualify
1978 did not qualify
1982 finals 2nd round
1986 fourth place
1990 finals 2nd round
1994 finals 2nd round

The Coach

Georges Leekens
Career: played for Houthalen, Dessel, Crossing, Brugge and Saint-Nicolas; coached Cercle, Anderlecht, Kortrijk, Brugge, Mechelen and Trabzonspor (Turkey), Cercle, Charleroi and Excelsior Mouscron.
Born: May 18, 1949
Appointed: January 1997

Star Performers

Filip Dewilde
Position: goalkeeper
Club: Anderlecht
Born: July 5, 1964

Franky Van der Elst
Position: defensive midfield
Club: Brugge
Born: April 30, 1961

Enzo Scifo
Position: midfield
Club: Anderlecht
Born: February 19, 1966

Luc Nilis
Position: forward
Club: PSV Eindhoven (Holland)
Born: May 25, 1967

Luis Oliveira
Position: forward
Club: Fiorentina (Italy)
Born: March 24, 1969

The Road to the Finals

Belgium 2–1 Turkey
San Marino 0–3 Belgium
Belgium 0–3 Holland
Wales 1–2 Belgium
Turkey 1–3 Belgium
Belgium 6–0 San Marino
Holland 3–1 Belgium
Belgium 3–2 Wales
Rep. of Ire 1–1 Belgium*
Belgium 2–1 Rep. of Ireland*
*Play-offs

SOUTH KOREA

Worthy to welcome the world

Group E

South Korea have reached the World Cup finals four times in a row – an Asian record – and will make it five in 2002, when they host the finals jointly with Japan.

South Korea's appearance will climax six remarkable years in the sporting history of a nation which, to much of the world, previously meant either armed conflict or economic explosion. All the varying elements of Korean life were brought together in the early 1990s by Chung Mong-joon, scion of the Hyundai corporation who moved up from federation president to the FIFA executive committee and led the campaign which earned Korea joint hosting rights for 2002.

The national team did not reach the international competitive stage until the 1948 Olympic Games and in 1954 they made their debut at the World Cup in Switzerland.

The experience was painful: Korea crashed 9–0 to Hungary and 7–0 to Turkey. But they soon established their credentials as soccer leaders in the Far East by winning the first two Asian Cups and creating a semi-professional championship, albeit organised among company teams.

In 1986 South Korea returned to the World Cup finals. They finished bottom of their first-round group but managed a 1–1 draw with Bulgaria and went down 3–1 to eventual champions Argentina. The Koreans benefited from the newly-constructed professional league and from the experience gained by senior men such as midfielder Cha Bum Kun in the German Bundesliga.

Close finishers

In 1990 South Korea were back but, despite the natural talent of players such as Kim Josung and Choi Soon Ho, they fell short of the second round. In the United States four years ago the Koreans went out with a bang, losing a dramatic last group match 3–2 to Cup-holders West Germany.

The potential evident then was confirmed when South Korea qualified easily for France, winning nine matches, drawing two and losing only one.

The high point of the qualifying campaign was the 2–1 victory in Tokyo last September. Korea's only defeat along the qualifying path was 2–0 at home to Japan, but it did not matter because they had already booked their ticket by thrashing Uzbekistan 5–1 two weeks earler.

In France, the Koreans will be pressing for that first finals victory for two specific reasons. They want to underline their right to play hosts in 2002, and they still regret that the only Korean victory in the World Cup was achieved by North Korea, who beat Italy at Middlesbrough in 1966.

As Cha Bum Kun said: 'It's time we left history where it belongs – in the past."

World Cup Record

1930	did not enter	**1970**	did not qualify
1934	did not enter	**1974**	did not qualify
1938	did not enter	**1978**	did not qualify
1950	did not enter	**1982**	did not qualify
1954	finals 1st rnd	**1986**	finals 1st rnd
1958	did not enter	**1990**	finals 1st rnd
1962	did not qualify	**1994**	finals 1st rnd
1966	did not enter		

The Coach

Cha Bum Kun
Career: played for Kyung Shin High School, Korea University, Korean Air Force, Eintracht Frankfurt (Germany), Bayern Leverkusen (Germany); coached Ulsan Hyundai.
Born: May 22, 1953
Appointed: January 1997

Star Performers

Kim Byung Ji
Position: goalkeeper
Club: Sangmoo (Korean army)
Born: April 8, 1970

Hong Myung Bo
Position: central defender
Club: Bellmare Hiratsuka (Japan)
Born: February 12, 1969

Ha Seok Ju
Position: midfield
Club: Ajoo University
Born: February 20, 1968

Ko Jung Woon
Position: forward
Club: Cerezo Osaka (Japan)
Born: June 27, 1966

Choi Yong Soo
Position: striker
Club: Sangmoo (army)
Born: September 10, 1973

The Road to the Finals

South Korea 3–0 Kazakhstan	Kazakhstan 1–1 South Korea
South Korea 2–1 Uzbekistan	Uzbekistan 1–5 South Korea
Japan 1–2 South Korea	South Korea 0–2 Japan
South Korea 3–0 UAE	UAE 0–2 South Korea

Far East powerhouse South Korea travel to Europe full of confidence in their abilities

MEXICO

Trying to end the European jinx

Group E

After 32 long years, Mexico are back at a "European" World Cup. The last time the top nation in Central and North America reached the finals was 1966, in England.

The Mexico team with former coach Bora Milutinovic, replaced after qualification

Mexican fans feared that a European World Cup automatically carried some sort of jinx. Mexico failed to overcome Haiti in the qualifying competition in 1974. Then, when two qualifying spots for CONCACAF appeared to hand qualification for Spain on a plate to Mexico in 1982, Honduras and El Salvador beat them to the punch.

But the most humiliating absence was that from Italy in 1990, when Mexico were barred after fielding ineligible players in a world youth event.

The federation, determined to make no mistake this time, went back to their most successful national coach, Bora Milutinovic. He had proved highly popular when Mexico hosted the finals – falling only to West Germany in a quarter-final shoot-out – in 1986. Once Mexico qualified for the 1998 finals, Milutinovic was replaced by another former national team boss, Manuel Lapuente.

CONCACAF has three representatives at the finals in France but Mexico always were favourites to top the final qualifying group. They had byes through the first three rounds. The semi-final stage was split into three round-robin groups and the Mexicans went through theirs after disposing of Jamaica, Honduras and St Vincent and the Grenadines – though they did suffer somewhat surprising defeats away to Honduras and eventual qualifiers Jamaica along the way.

Flamboyant Campos

As the final round wound to a conclusion, Mexico secured the point they needed from a goalless draw against the United States. The fans were not happy, because the Americans had been beaten on each of 17 previous visits, but qualifying was the priority. So seriously did the federation take the demand to reach France that the league championship play-off finals were postponed to clear the decks for the last two World Cup matches.

Mexico will be among the most technically gifted contenders, with goalkeeper Jorge Campos the flashiest of all. FIFA may be called in to rule on the dazzling outfits which delight his fans in Mexico and the United States, where he plays for LA Galaxy.

Campos provides Lapuente with a most unusual option. He is not only a talented goalkeeper but also has played in attack on varous occasions with great success. His clubs have rescued games by putting on a substitute keeper and sending Campos up front – with a change of shirt, of course.

Ramon Ramirez was voted the most outstanding left-back at the last Copa America, when Mexico finished third, and Luis Garcia and Alberto Garcia Aspe are highly-skilled midfielders.

World Cup Record

1930	finals 1st round	**1970**	finals 1st round
1934	did not enter	**1974**	failed to qualify
1938	did not enter	**1978**	finals 1st round
1950	finals 1st round	**1982**	failed to qualify
1954	finals 1st round	**1986**	quarter-finals
1958	finals 1st round	**1990**	suspended
1962	finals 1st round	**1994**	finals 2nd round
1966	finals 1st round		

The Coach

Manuel Lapuente
Career: played for Puebla; coached Puebla and Necaxa and the Mexican national team in 1991–92.
Born: March 17, 1944
Appointed: November 1997

Star Performers

Jorge Campos
Position: goalkeeper
Clubs: Cruz Azul (Mex) and LA Galaxy (US)
Born: October 15, 1966

Ramon Ramirez
Position: defender
Club: Guadalajara
Born: December 5, 1969

Alberto Garcia Aspe
Position: midfield
Club: America
Born: May 11, 1967

Luis Garcia
Position: midfield
Club: Atlante
Born: June 1, 1969

Luis Roberto Alves "Zague"
Position: forward
Club: America
Born: May 23, 1967

The Road to the Finals

Mexico 4–0 Canada	Mexico 5–0 El Salvador
Costa Rica 0–0 Mexico	Canada 2–2 Mexico
Mexico 6–0 Jamaica	Mexico 0–0 United States
United States 2–2 Mexico	Mexico 3–3 Costa Rica
El Salvador 0–1 Mexico	Jamaica 0–0 Mexico

The country no other dare ignore

Group F

Germany will always be among the World Cup favourites – whenever and wherever the finals may happen to be.

Germany won Euro 96, but can they top European domination?

Clearly, neighbouring France is an ideal venue for the three-times winners to bid to regain the world crown they lost four years ago in the United States.

Now Germany travel the short distance proud of their status as the champions of Europe, secured with that dramatic golden-goal victory over the Czech Republic at Wembley in June 1996.

But the signs from the 1998 World Cup qualifying campaign are that the national team may not be quite the consistent force of previous World Cups.

Fortunately, the manner in which their group rivals took points off each other meant that Germany came to their last game needing only a draw to secure qualification. Even then, remarkably, the Germans found themselves a goal down to the unfancied Albanians, at home, and needed a two-goal rescue act from Oliver Bierhoff to turn the game around.

The tactical model for the German national team remains much the same as ever. Coach Berti Vogts, a World Cup-winner in 1974, is likely to rely on a sweeper, two marking central defenders and a five-man midfield.

Plenty of experience

In goal Vogts is spoiled for choice between Andy Köpke, one of the Euro 96 heroes, and Bayern Munich's Oliver Kahn. Central defence continues to be dominated by Dortmund's Jürgen Kohler and Matthias Sammer though the latter, the 1996 European Footballer of the Year, missed most of the first half of the season because of knee problems. Andy Möller and Thomas Hässler will bring all their experience to bear in midfield with the support of younger players such as Christian Ziege, who missed the 1996 European Championship through injury.

Up front Vogts again appears spoiled for choice. Veteran skipper Jürgen Klinsmann struggled for goals in 1997 but is determined to enjoy a memorable last finals before he retires. Alongside him Vogts can choose between Bierhoff – match-winning substitute of Euro 96, – former East German internationals Kirsten and Olaf Marschall, as well as the South African-born Sean Dundee.

Certainly Germany will be well organized. At Euro 96, they left little to chance, as Vogts remembered the semi-final shoot-out victory. "I told Andy Möller he would take the sixth penalty for us and he would win the game with it".

Rivals underestimate Germany, with such a record and depth of talent, at their peril.

World Cup Record

1930	did not enter	**1970**	third place
1934	third place	**1974**	champions
1938	finals 1st rnd	**1978**	finals 2nd rnd
1950	did not enter	**1982**	runners-up
1954	champions	**1986**	runners-up
1958	fourth place	**1990**	champions
1962	quarter-finals	**1994**	quarter-finals
1966	runners-up		

The Coach

Berti Vogts
Career: played for Borussia Mönchengladbach; coached the German youth and under-21 squads.
Born: December 30, 1946
Appointed: August 1990

Star Performers

Matthias Sammer
Position: sweeper
Club: Borussia Dortmund
Born: September 5, 1967

Jürgen Kohler
Position: centre back
Club: Borussia Dortmund
Born: October 6, 1965

Andy Möller
Position: midfield
Club: Borussia Dortmund
Born: September 2, 1967

Jürgen Klinsmann
Position: striker
Club: Tottenham Hotspur (England)
Born: July 30, 1964

Oliver Bierhoff
Position: centre-forward
Club: Udinese (Italy)
Born: May 1, 1968

The Road to the Finals

Armenia 1–5 Germany	Ukraine 0–0 Germany
Germany 1–1 N Ireland	N Ireland 1–3 Germany
Portugal 0–0 Germany	Germany 1–1 Portugal
Albania 2–3 Germany	Germany 4–0 Armenia
Germany 2–0 Ukraine	Germany 4–3 Albania

USA

Making soccer a major sport

Group F

According to national coach Steve Sampson, the World Cup finals have begun. Not in France but in Burnaby, British Columbia, back on November 9 last year.

Despite recent successes the United States public has yet to take to football in numbers

That was how Sampson sought to motivate his players for their decisive qualifying tie against Canada. In the event the Americans won 3–0 and thus appear in the finals for the third successive time. Not bad for a nation whose relationship with soccer is still an object of suspicion in much of the world.

The Americans cruised serenely through the early qualifying stages, but the final round was not so simple.

A goalless draw in Jamaica and a 3–0 home win over Canada was the right start but points went missing in the next three games. Then a 1–0 defeat of Costa Rica brought qualification back into view, and though a draw against Jamaica was disappointing, a 0–0 result in Mexico was a moral victory. They had lost all their 17 previous visits, and came away with a draw despite playing for an hour without the sent-off Jeff Agoos.

Winning in Canada would have appeared less of a challenge had the US been at full strength, but not only was Agoos absent so were Tab Ramos and Kasey Keller (injured) and John Harkes (also suspended). In the circumstances, a 3–0 win was remarkable.

It is more than a century since soccer was introduced to the US. The Americans sent a good team to the inaugural World Cup in Uruguay in 1930 and reached the semi-finals. In 1934 the US again went to the World Cup finals but crashed 7–1 to Italy in their first and only match. No wonder it was such a shock when they beat a powerful England 1–0 in Brazil in 1950.

Ideal springboard

The Americans took 40 years to return – but they were years in which the Americans persuaded FIFA to let them host the World Cup in 1994. This was the first time the event had gone to a country where soccer was not the No 1 sport. The finals were a great success and provided an ideal springboard for the launch of Major League Soccer.

Not all the US World Cup qualifying regulars play MLS. Goalkeeper Kasey Keller, for instance, racks up the air miles flying to and from his duties in England with Premiership club Leicester City. Veterans Marcelo Balboa, Alexi Lalas and Paul Caligiuri have remained key members of the defensive set-up, despite the change of coach when Sampson took over from Bora Milutinovic after the 1994 finals.

As Sampson explained: "Getting to the World Cup finals means we can continue trying to bring in those American sports fans who are sitting on the fence – and turn soccer into a major sport in the States."

World Cup Record

1930 semi-finals
1934 finals 1st rnd
1938 did not enter
1950 finals 1st rnd
1954 did not qualify
1958 did not qualify
1962 did not qualify
1966 did not qualify
1970 did not qualify
1974 did not qualify
1978 did not qualify
1982 did not qualify
1986 did not qualify
1990 finals 1st rnd
1994 finals 2nd rnd

The Coach

Steve Sampson
Career: played college soccer with UCLA and San Jose State; coached Santa Clara before he joined the USSF coaching staff.
Born: January 19, 1957
Appointed: August 1995

Star Performers

Kasey Keller
Position: goalkeeper
Club: Leicester City (England)
Born: November 27, 1969

Alexi Lalas
Position: defender
Club: New England Revolution
Born: June 1, 1970

John Harkes
Position: midfield
Club: DC United
Born: September 3, 1967

Tab Ramos
Position: midfield
Club: New Jersey/New York MetroStars
Born: September 21, 1966

Eric Wynalda
Position: forward
Club: San Jose Clash
Born: June 9, 1969

The Road to the Finals

Jamaica 0–0 USA
USA 3–0 Canada
Costa Rica 3–2 USA
USA 2–2 Mexico
El Salvador 1–1 USA
USA 1–0 Costa Rica
USA 1–1 Jamaica
Mexico 0–0 USA
Canada 0–3 USA
USA 4–2 El Salvador

YUGOSLAVIA

Back on the biggest stage

Group F

Yugoslavia are back at the World Cup finals – a penalty shoot-out, eight years and a civil war since they last appeared on world football's greatest stage.

Yugoslavia reached the finals after trouncing Hungary in the play-off

That was in Florence, in the 1990 quarter-finals, when Yugoslavia included Croatia, Bosnia and Slovenia – now all independent nations on the political and sporting maps. Yugoslavia now means the so-called rump states of Serbia and Montenegro, but judging from the way they wrapped up their qualifying campaign, the Slavs will be as dangerous as ever.

They finished second behind Spain in their group, leaving Slovakia and the Czech Republic – 1996 European Championship runners-up – in their wake. Then, away to Hungary in the play-offs, Yugoslavia won by a sensational 7–1. Hat-trick hero Predrag Mijatovic, from Real Madrid, had no doubt about his team's ambition. He said: "We prepared for this as though we were to meet Brazil. We want to show the world what they missed during our absence. Now we will be the wonder of France."

The new generation

Only two of the Yugoslav players against Hungary survived from the team beaten on penalties by Argentina in 1990: midfielder Dragan Stojkovic and forward Dejan Savicevic, now seniors inspiring a new generation of players who have made their name on the club stage across Europe but have been barred from the World Cup and European Championship.

Yugoslavia are "Europe's Argentina" – the continent's greatest exporter of playing and coaching talent. That image has been shining since 1930, when Yugoslavia were one of only four European nations to attend the first World Cup, in Uruguay. Since then they have qualified six times and achieved their best finish in 1962, when fourth in Chile.

For many members of the current team, this World Cup will be both their first and last. As Savicevic says: "That's why we tried so hard to reach France – and that's why we'll play a major role when there."

A solid defence is the foundation for what is potentially one of the most powerful midfield and attacking units at the finals, with danger created from the back by Stojkovic, Vladimir Jugovic – a European club champion in 1996 with Juventus – and free-kick specialist Sinisa Mihajlovic.

In front of them, teasing opposing defences with their pace, close control and general mischief are Savicevic – Champions Cup-Winners medalist with Milan – and Mijatovic. Leading the line is Savo Milosevic, successful with his country but struggling with English club Aston Villa.

"I always believed that this generation of players would be the one to bring us back to the World Cup," says coach Slobodan Santrac. "They deserved it – they earned it."

World Cup Record

1930	semi-finals	**1970**	did not qualify
1934	did not qualify	**1974**	finals 2nd rnd
1938	did not qualify	**1978**	did not qualify
1950	finals 1st rnd	**1982**	finals 1st rnd
1954	quarter-finals	**1986**	did not qualify
1958	quarter-finals	**1990**	quarter-finals
1962	fourth place	**1994**	did not enter
1966	did not qualify		

The Coach

Slobodan Santrac
Career: played for OFK Belgrade, Partizan Belgrade, Grasshopper (Switz.), Galenika; coached Yugoslavia youth and under-21 squads.
Born: July 1, 1946
Appointed: July 1993

Star Performers

Vladimir Jugovic
Position: midfield
Club: Lazio (Italy)
Born: August 30, 1969

Sinisa Mihajlovic
Position: defence/midfield
Club: Sampdoria (Italy)
Born: February 20, 1969

Dragan Stojkovic
Position: midfield
Club: Grampus 8 (Japan)
Born: March 3, 1965

Dejan Savicevic
Position: forward
Club: Milan (Italy)
Born: September 15, 1966

Predrag Mijatovic
Position: forward
Club: Real Madrid (Spain)
Born: January 19, 1969

The Road to the Finals

Yugoslavia 3–1 Faroe Is.
Yugoslavia 6–0 Malta
Faroe Is. 1–8 Yugoslavia
Yugoslavia 1–0 Czech Rep.
Spain 2–0 Yugoslavia
Czech Rep. 1–2 Yugoslavia
Yugoslavia 1–1 Spain
Yugoslavia 2–0 Slovakia
Slovakia 1–1 Yugoslavia
Malta 0–5 Yugoslavia
Hungary 1–7 Yugoslavia*
Yugoslavia 5–0 Hungary*

*Play-offs

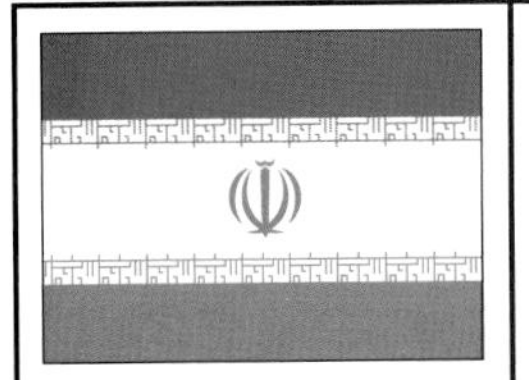

IRAN

Records all the way

Group F

Iran return to the finals for the first time since 1978 with three proud claims to their regained fame.

Kharim Bagheri was the most successful individual in the worldwide qualifying competition, scoring 19 goals in 17 matches. Iran achieved a single-match record score, thrashing Maldives 17–0, and became highest overall scorers with 57 goals.

The last two goals – against Australia in the last 14 minutes of the climactic play-off in Melbourne – were the most vital of all. Against all the apparent odds, Iran rescued a draw which earned victory on away goals and lifted them into the finals.

That Iran even got as far as the lucky losers' play-off was remarkable, considering the fact that they had failed to win any of their last six matches.

The Iranians appeared within reach of France after racing into the leadership by decisive victories over China and Qatar and draws with Saudi Arabia and Kuwait. A further win over China enabled coach Mohammad Mayeli Kohan to shrug off criticism of his tactics and training methods.

But the criticism grew more strident after Iran lost 1–0 to Saudi Arabia and were held goalless at home by Kuwait. Several players threatened to walk out after a further row. Mayeli Kohan was dismissed and "Badu" Vierra, who had been in charge of the Olympic team, was promoted caretaker manager, albeit too late to make any difference against Qatar. Iran duly went down 2–0 and had to settle for second place behind Saudi Arabia in the group.

That meant a play-off against Japan in Malaysia, with the winners going to the finals and the losers playing off against Australia. Midway through the second half Iran led 2–1, only to lose 3–2 in the last minute of extra time.

The first leg of the Asia-Oceania play-off was in front of 120,000 in Tehran, and a 1–1 draw appeared to hand control to Australia, who led 2–0 in the second leg in front of 85,000. But Bagheri and Azizi capitalized on two defensive howlers to equalise and Iran qualified on away goals.

Top spot in Asia

Iran did not play their first official international until 1950 – a 6–1 defeat in Turkey – but neverthless went on to become the top Asian football nation, well worth their first appearance at the World Cup finals, in Argentina in 1978. They beat Australia and Kuwait on the way, and distinguished themselves further by forcing a 1–1 draw against Scotland at the finals.

Iran did not even enter the World Cup in 1982 and 1986 and when they did return, all that experience from the 1970s had evaporated. Now, at last, Iran are back to make up for lost time.

Iran's comeback from 2–0 down to draw with Australia earned them their place at the finals

World Cup Record

1930 did not enter
1934 did not enter
1938 did not enter
1950 did not enter
1954 did not enter
1958 did not enter
1962 did not enter
1966 did not enter
1970 did not enter
1974 did not qualify
1978 finals 1st rnd
1982 did not enter
1986 did not enter
1990 did not qualify
1994 did not qualify

The Coach

Tomislav Ivic
Career: coached Hajduk Split, Anderlecht, Galatasaray, Avellino, Panathinaikos, Dinamo Zagreb, FC Porto, Paris St-Germain, Atletico Madrid, Marseille, Benfica, Croatia, United Arab Emirates.
Born: June 30, 1933
Appointed: January 1998

Star Performers

Ahmadreza Abedzadeh
Position: goalkeeper
Club: Pirouzi
Born: 1966

Mohammed Khakpour
Position: defender
Club: Geylang United (Singapore)
Born: 1969

Khodadad Azizi
Position: midfield
Club: Koln (Germany)
Born: June 22, 1971

Kharim Bagheri
Position: midfield
Club: Arminia Bielefeld (Germany)
Born: February 20, 1974

Ali Daei
Position: forward
Club: Arminia Bielefeld (Germany)
Born: March 21, 1969

The Road to the Finals

China 2–4 Iran
Iran 1–1 Saudi Arabia
Kuwait 1–1 Iran
Iran 3–0 Qatar
Iran 4–1 China
Saudi Arabia 1–0 Iran
Iran 0–0 Kuwait
Qatar 2–0 Iran
Japan 3–2 Iran*
Iran 1–1 Australia*
Australia 2–2 Iran*
*Play-offs

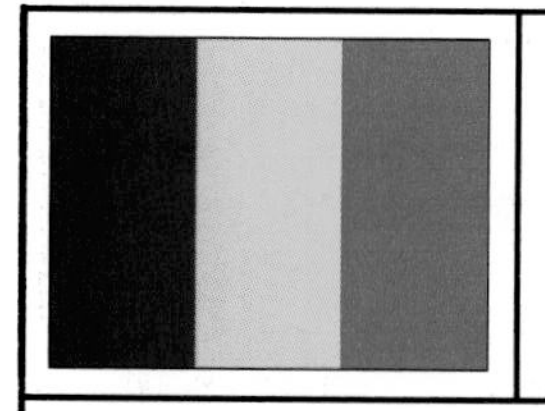

ROMANIA

Competitive all the way through

Group G

Romania knew they were going to the World Cup finals more than a year before the scheduled start of the extravaganza in France.

A 1–0 win over the Irish Republic in April 1997 virtually guaranteed them the right to start planning for the finals. The three points delighted their fans and surprised observers who thought Romania were way past their best.

But the World Cup always has held an extra-special place in Romanian affections – ever since they were one of the four European nations who competed at the inaugural finals in Uruguay.

They did so thanks to the enthusiasm of King Carol, who paid the players while they were away. Romania were eliminated in the first round in 1930, 1934 and 1938. Thus it was nearly 50 years before they asserted themselves on the international stage.

Since then, however, there has been no holding the ambitious footballers of this Balkan state.

No luck in shootouts

Romania reached the second round of the 1990 World Cup, only to lose on a penalty shoot-out to the Republic of Ireland after a goalless 120 minutes

Four years later they went one round better before again losing on penalties, to Sweden. Gheorge Hagi has long been their inspiration, superbly supported by defensive midfielder Gheorghe "Gica" Popescu. Anghel Iordanescu, a member of Steaua's European Cup-winning team in 1986, had become coach in '93, and in '96 he took Romania to the European Championship finals which turned into a disaster. The linesmen and referee did not see a shot against France cross the line and go back into play, and the price was first-round elimination.

The federation could have thrown out the coaching staff and half the squad, but they kept faith in the men who had served so well, even persuading Iordanescu to resist foreign offers and sign a contract extension. He had more than earned it by the manner in which his constantly evolving team dominated their qualifying group.

Romania opened with a 3–0 win over Lithuania, victories in Iceland and Macedonia, home to Liechtenstein, in Lithuania and then – decisively – home to Ireland, without losing a goal. Remarkably, anchor man Popescu emerged as top scorer.

He and fellow stalwarts such as Hagi and striker Ilie Dumitrescu underwent various career crises at club level after the 1994 World Cup, but took the opportunity to rebuild their confidence and international reputations. Romania will not only be one of the most competitive of World Cup contenders, but one of the most experienced.

Romania's veteran squad will have a great chance after earning a top-seed rank

World Cup Record

1930	finals 1st round	**1970**	finals 1st round
1934	finals 1st round	**1974**	did not qualify
1938	finals 1st round	**1978**	did not qualify
1950	did not enter	**1982**	did not qualify
1954	did not qualify	**1986**	did not qualify
1958	did not qualify	**1990**	finals 2nd round
1962	withdrew	**1994**	quarter finals
1966	did not qualify		

The Coach

Anghel Iordanescu
Career: played for Steaua Bucharest, player-coach at Anorthosis Famagusta (Cyprus); coached Steaua Bucharest.
Born: March 4, 1950
Appointed: August 1993

Star Performers

Bogdan Stelea
Position: goalkeeper
Club: Steaua Bucharest
Born: December 5, 1967

Dan Petrescu
Position: fullback/midfield
Club: Chelsea (England)
Born: December 22, 1967

Gheorghe Popescu
Position: defensive midfield
Club: Galatasaray (Turkey)
Born: October 9, 1967

Gheorghe Hagi
Position: midfield
Club: Galatasaray (Turkey)
Born: February 5, 1965

Adrian Ilie
Position: forward
Club: Galatasaray (Turkey)
Born: April 20, 1974

The Road to the Finals

Romania 3–0 Lithuania
Iceland 0–4 Romania
Macedonia 0–3 Romania
Lithuania 0–1 Romania
Romania 8–0 Liechtenstein
Romania 1–0 Rep. of Ireland
Romania 4–2 Macedonia
Liechtenstein 1–8 Romania
Romania 4–0 Iceland
Rep. of Ireland 1–1 Romania

COLOMBIA

Determined to make amends

Group G

A special welcome awaits Colombia back at the World Cup finals after the sad events of four years ago.

The Colombians will hope World Cup 1998 is less traumatic than 1994

The Colombian team arrived in the United States packed with colourful individuals and tipped as potential winners by no less an authority than Pele. But all they took from USA '94 was tragedy. Death threats to players wrecked morale, and defender Pablo Escobar was shot dead within days of the team's return after first-round elimination.

Now Colombia are in the finals again, determined to atone for their errors and, above all, to repay their debt to the memory of Escobar, whose only "crime" was to deflect the ball into his own net in a defeat by the United States.

Introduced by English sailors in 1924, Colombian football has never been dull, and it has flourished since 1948 when new clubs such as Millonarios launched the legendary pirate championship.

Team of characters

After missing out on the 1986 World Cup Finals, Colombia finished third in the 1987 Copa America and frizzy-haired midfielder Carlos Valderrama was elected South American Footballer of the Year, the first Colombian to collect the accolade.

Atletico Nacional of Medellin then emerged as the top team in South America, winning the Copa Libertadores in 1989. National boss Francisco Maturana was the club coach, and the following year he used Atletico Nacional as the backbone of his side at the World Cup finals in Italy. Colombia reached the second round before a mistake by flamboyant goalkeeper Rene Orlando Higuita condemned them to defeat by Cameroon.

They made a perfect start to the 1998 qualifying competition by defeating Paraguay 1–0 with a goal from Tino Asprilla. The England-based striker followed that with the opening goal of a 3–1 home over Uruguay, two in a 4–1 defeat of Chile and the only goal in Ecuador.

However, just as qualification was looking a formality complacency set in. The Colombians lost three matches, drew one and lost another. But just in time they recovered to beat Ecuador 1–0 and Bolivia 3–0. Veterans Valderrama and Anthony De Avila were the heroes now, De Avila scoring in both matches and Valderrama reasserting his midfield command against the Bolivians in his record 101st international.

A 1–0 win over Venezuela sealed the place in the finals with a game to spare. The players and coaching staff celebrated long into the night. They have a score to settle with football history.

World Cup Record

1930	did not enter	**1970**	did not qualify
1934	did not enter	**1974**	did not qualify
1938	did not enter	**1978**	did not qualify
1950	did not enter	**1982**	did not qualify
1954	did not enter	**1986**	did not qualify
1958	did to qualify	**1990**	finals 2nd round
1962	finals 1st round	**1994**	finals first round
1966	did not qualify		

The Coach

Hernan Dario Gomez
Career: played for Nacional Medellin; coached Nacional, then the Colombian junior team before becoming national assistant.
Born: February 3, 1956
Appointed: August 1994

Star Performers

Wilmer Cabrera
Position: full-back
Club: America Cali
Born: September 15, 1967

Fredy Rincon
Position: midfield
Club: Palmeiras (Brz)
Born: August 14, 1966

Carlos Valderrama
Position: midfield
Club: Miami Fusion (USA)
Born: September 2, 1961

Faustino Asprilla
Position: striker
Club: Newcastle United (England)
Born: November 10, 1969

Anthony De Avila
Position: forward
Club: America Cali
Born: December 21, 1962

The Road to the Finals

Colombia 1–0 Paraguay	Paraguay 2–1 Colombia
Peru 1–1 Colombia	Colombia 0–1 Peru
Colombia 3–1 Uruguay	Uruguay 1–1 Colombia
Colombia 4–1 Chile	Chile 4–1 Colombia
Ecuador 0–1 Colombia	Colombia 1–0 Ecuador
Bolivia 2–2 Colombia	Colombia 3–0 Bolivia
Venezuela 0–2 Colombia	Colombia 1–0 Venezuela
Colombia 0–1 Argentina	Argentina 1–1 Colombia

ENGLAND

Will it be gloomy or glorious?

Group G

England carry around almost too much historical baggage for their own good when it comes to international competition.

England won Le Tournoi in 1997. A year on, the World Cup is the target

Glenn Hoddle was on the upward swing of his learning curve, after succeeding Terry Venables as boss after Euro 96, when England faced their toughest group rivals, Italy, at Wembley in February 1997. A break-away goal from Gianfranco Zola condemned England to a defeat which provoked all sorts of recriminations and gloomy forecasts that even reaching the finals was beyond reach – never mind what might happen there.

Then, after Italy dropped silly points and England secured the goalless draw in Rome which sent Hoddle's men direct to the finals, the talk was all about prospects of carrying off the golden trophy.

Not much to show

In Venables and his successor Hoddle, England have benefited from coaches who understand that only a mixture of traditional English virtues (power and high morale) and continental values (technique and tactical awareness) can carry the day on the World Cup stage.

England's displays at Euro 96, were a revelation – above all the thrilling manner of the 4–1 thrashing of Holland in the first round.

The nucleus of that team, and the so-called "Christmas Tree" tactical formation, offered Hoddle the foundations to build upon.

Shearer – main man

But, for all the qualities evident in defence and midfield, it is on Alan Shearer's goal-scoring talents that England's World Cup challenge will stand or fall. Shearer is generally accepted as Europe's most dangerous centre-forward.

The Newcastle striker does not have the flashy finesse of a Ronaldo or the lurking menace of a Gabriel Batistuta, but a record of 16 goals in 35 internationals tells its own story. Shearer's nose for a goal chance earned him world record transfer status when he left Blackburn Rovers for Newcastle for £15 million.

Shearer has not had the greatest fortune with injuries and he missed most of the first half of the 1997–98 campaign after damaging ankle ligaments. But, as he observed, "that just means I'll be fresher than most of the rest when it comes to the World Cup finals."

There's a lot of England supporters who hope he is right.

World Cup Record

1930 did not enter
1934 did not enter
1938 did not enter
1950 finals 1st rnd
1954 quarter-finals
1958 finals 1st rnd
1962 quarter-finals
1966 champions
1970 quarter-finals
1974 did not qualify
1978 did not qualify
1982 finals 2nd rnd
1986 quarter-finals
1990 fourth place
1994 did not qualify

The Coach

Glenn Hoddle
Career: played for Tottenham, Monaco, Chelsea and Swindon; coached Swindon and Chelsea.
Born: October 27, 1957
Appointed: July 1996

Star Performers

David Seaman
Position: goalkeeper
Club: Arsenal
Born: September 19, 1963

Gareth Southgate
Position: defender
Club: Aston Villa
Born: September 3, 1970

Paul Gascoigne
Position: midfield
Club: Rangers (Scotland)
Born: May 27, 1967

Paul Ince
Position: midfielder
Club: Liverpool
Born: October 21, 1967

David Beckham
Position: midfield
Club: Manchester United
Born: May 2, 1975

Alan Shearer
Position: centre-forward
Club: Newcastle United
Born: August 13, 1970

The Road to the Finals

Moldova 0–3 England
England 2–1 Poland
Georgia 0–2 England
England 0–1 Italy
England 2–0 Georgia
Poland 0–2 England
England 4–0 Moldova
Italy 0–0 England

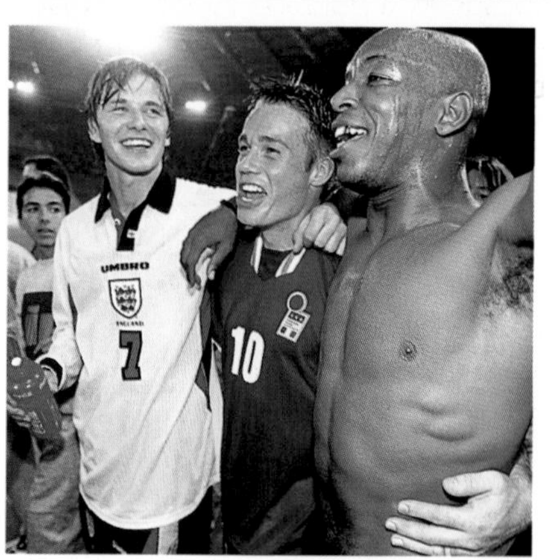

David Beckham (7), Graham Le Saux (10) and Ian Wright rejoice in Rome

TUNISIA

A return in the right place

Group G

Tunisia are back at the World Cup finals for the first time in 20 years – a surprisingly long absence considering the potential they displayed at the finals in Argentina, and their long soccer history.

Tunisia conceded only one goal in their final qualifying group matches

They were the first African nation, after Egypt, to reach the final rounds of the Olympic Games, and were among the earliest and most enthusiastic supporters of both the African Nations Cup and the continental club cups.

Now coach Henryk Kasperczak and his team intend to make up for lost time. And where better than France, which provided the Tunisians with their initial taste for the game? French colonial officials took the first footballs to Tunis at the start of the century, a national championship was founded in 1921 and a knock-out cup a year later.

In 1960, Tunisia, remarkably, reached the final rounds of the Olympic Games soccer tournament in Rome. They then became the first French-language North African nation to enter the African Nations Cup and finished runners-up, as hosts, in 1965.

Their star player and midfield general was skipper Majid Chetali, who re-emerged in 1978 when he managed the Tunisians to the World Cup finals in Argentina. They sprang a major shock with a 3–1 victory over Mexico, losing only 1–0 to Poland and securing a 0–0 draw with defending Cup-holders West Germany… who pipped them to a second-round place by that one point.

Tunisia began the 1998 campaign at the preliminary stage. Rwanda were despatched 3–1 away and 2–0 at home to set up a group which featured Tunisia, George Weah's Liberia, Namibia and Egypt.

Chokri chokes crowd

Kasperczak, an old World Cup hero with Poland, based his tactical system on solid discipline in defence. It was highly effective. Tunisia won five of their six group matches, scored only 10 goals but conceded a miserly one. Goalkeeper Chokri El Ouaer and his fellow defenders proved especially frustrating for the Egyptians. Tunisia won 1–0 at home and drew 0–0 away. The match in Cairo, in front of a hostile 100,000 crowd, proved decisive.

Playing hero of Tunisia's triumphant campaign was attacking midfielder Adel Sellimi, an international in 1991 aged 18, who had achieved attention in the Tunisian side that finished African Nations' runners-up to South Africa in 1996, after which he transferred to French club Nantes.

Up front, Tunisia will look for goals to Ben Slimane from another French club, Marseille Kasperczak, meanwhile, will try to keep his players' feet on the ground. As he said: "In Africa we have become the team everyone wants to beat and that's a difficult challenge to meet."

World Cup Record

1930 did not enter
1934 did not enter
1938 did not enter
1950 did not enter
1954 did not enter
1958 did not enter
1962 did not qualify
1966 did not enter
1970 did not qualify
1974 did not qualify
1978 finals 1st rnd
1982 did not qualify
1986 did not qualify
1990 did not qualify
1994 did not qualify

The Coach

Henryk Kasperczak
Career: played for Stal Mielec (Poland), Metz (France) and the Poland team who finished third at the 1974 World Cup; coached Metz, Saint-Etienne, Strasbourg, Matra Racing, Montpellier, Lille (all in France) and Ivory Coast national team.
Born: July 10, 1946
Appointed: June 1994

Star Performers

Chokri El Ouaer
Position: goalkeeper
Club: Esperance Tunis
Born: August 15, 1966

Sami Trabelsi
Position: defender
Club: CS Sfax
Born: February 4, 1968

Zoubeir Beya
Position: midfield
Club: Etoile Sahel
Born: May 15, 1971

Adel Sellimi
Position: midfield
Club: Nantes (France)
Born: November 16, 1972

Ben Slimane
Position: forward
Club: Marseille (France)
Born: January 1, 1974

The Road to the Finals

Liberia 0–1 Tunisia
Tunisia 1–0 Egypt
Namibia 1–2 Tunisia
Tunisia 2–0 Liberia
Egypt 0–0 Tunisia
Tunisia 4–0 Namibia

ARGENTINA

At their best in a crisis

Group H

The abiding image of Argentina at the World Cup is one of controversy – of a team who carry their fanatical supporters through every emotion as they face the challenge with a mixture of skill, style and ruthless application.

In 1986, when Argentina won the World Cup for a second time, Daniel Passarella was merely a reserve. But France will see the captain of the 1978 World Cup winning team make a comeback on to the main stage as Argentina's national coach.

Passarella knows plenty about top-level international football. To the job of national coach he brings a knowledge of football – its technique, tactics and psychology – which mixes the best of the game's old and new worlds. A strict disciplinarian, Passarella first demanded his players had short hair, but later he relented.

Keepers weepers

The qualifying effort began well enough with a win over Bolivia. But then came defeat in Ecuador, a goalless draw with Peru and a home draw against Paraguay. A 5–2 away win over Venezuela offered Passarella little respite, because they were the weakest team in the group. Then came further disappointment with a 1–1 home draw against Chile.

Passarella's problem position was goalkeeper. Ignacio Carlos Gonzalez was Argentina's fifth in seven games when he kept crucial clean sheets in a 0–0 draw with Uruguay and 1–0 win in Colombia. Then Gonzalez took heavy blame for a 2–1 defeat in Bolivia and keeper No. 6 – Carlos Roa – was summoned.

At last Passarella had found a talisman. Ecuador, Peru, Paraguay, Venezuela and Chile were all beaten. Five successive wins meant that Argentina had secured their place in the finals.

Hidden talent

Although one of Argentina's star players, Gabriel Batistuta, was omitted for the closing stages of the qualifying campaign, the coach let it be known that "Batigol" – as he is known – would be one of the first names on his squad sheet when deciding the 22 players who will go the finals in France. The striker, who is based in Italy, is one of the world's most feared forwards.

Anyone who underrates Argentina solely on the basis of their somewhat scrappy qualifying campaign should think again. When it comes to the crunch, Argentina, one of the greatest teams in the world, have made a habit of pulling rabbits from the hat.

Argentina will be sure to field a winning team for the World Cup finals

World Cup Record

1930	runners-up	**1970**	did not qualify
1934	did not enter	**1974**	finals 2nd rnd
1938	withdrew	**1978**	champions
1950	withdrew	**1982**	finals 2nd rnd
1954	did not enter	**1986**	champions
1958	finals 1st rnd	**1990**	runners-up
1962	finals 1st rnd	**1994**	finals 2nd rnd
1966	quarter-finals		

The Coach

Daniel Passarella
Career: played for River Plate and Internazionale (Italy); coached River Plate.
Born: May 25, 1953
Appointed: September 1994

Star Performers

Juan Sebastian Veron
Position: midfield
Club: Sampdoria (Italy)
Born: March 9, 1975

Diego Simeone
Position: midfielder
Club: Internazionale (Italy)
Born: April 28, 1970

Ariel Ortega
Position: midfield
Club: Valencia (Spain)
Born: March 4, 1974

Gabriel Batistuta
Position: centre-forward
Club: Fiorentina (Italy)
Born: February 1, 1969

Hernan Crespo
Position: forward
Club: Parma (Italy)
Born: July 5, 1975

The Road to the Finals

Argentina 3–1 Bolivia	Bolivia 2–1 Argentina
Ecuador 2–0 Argentina	Argentina 2–1 Ecuador
Peru 0–0 Argentina	Argentina 2–0 Peru
Argentina 1–1 Paraguay	Paraguay 1–2 Argentina
Venezuela 2–5 Argentina	Argentina 2–0 Venezuela
Argentina 1–1 Chile	Chile 1–2 Argentina
Uruguay 0–0 Argentina	Argentina 0–0 Uruguay
Colombia 0–1 Argentina	Argentina 1–1 Colombia

JAPAN

Learning at lightning speed

A golden goal proved to be exactly that on November 16, 1997 when Japan defeated Iran in a play-off at Johor Bahru, Malaysia, to reach the World Cup finals for the first time.

Japan are ready and waiting for their first ever visit to the World Cup finals

Japan had entered the showdown in a state of high tension. Four years earlier an injury-time goal had denied them a place in the World Cup finals and upset the carefully-planned strategy launching of professional soccer in the Land of the Rising Sun.

Once again, Japan were so close to a first appearance in the finals. They had teetered on the brink of elimination: only an against-the-odds victory, 2–0 away to their old rivals – and World Cup 2002 partners – South Korea kept the dream alive.

Ultimately Japan finished second behind the Koreans and entered the play-off with Iran, runners-up behind Saudi Arabia in the other group.

New manager Takeshi Okada saw Masashi Nakayama shoot Japan ahead but Iran equalised and then went 2–1 up. Then Okada made the first of two remarkably successful decisions, sending on Shoji Jo, who struck the 75th-minute equaliser. At the start of extra time Okada sent on another substitute, Masayuki Okano, who turned from perpetual reserve to national hero when, with one minute remaining, he scored the winning goal.

That set off celebrations across the nation. Millions had watched on giant outdoor screens, and Prime Minister Ryutaro Hashimoto invited journalists into his office to share the excitement.

Japan's campaign had started almost a decade earlier when senior football, political and business leaders drew up the blueprint to launch professional football. The fledgling J. League was launched in 1993. The clubs were all new, created by a mixture of major corporations and local authorities.

World Cup 2002

Since then the Japanese have waged a lively campaign to build their soccer reputation. The national team took part impressively in a four-nation tournament in England in 1995 and the crowning glory off the field came when Japan and South Korea were awarded joint hosting rights to the 2002 World Cup.

One of the key figures in the team Japan will send to France is a Brazilian, Wagner Lopes from Bellmare Hiratsuka. Other leading figures will include goalkeeper Yoskikatsu Kawaguchi and veteran centre-back Masami Ihara, a former Asian Footballer of the Year. Okada says: "For us, being at the finals is what matters most. We have a lot to learn but we are learning – fast."

World Cup Record

1930 did not enter
1934 did not enter
1938 did not enter
1950 did not enter
1954 did not qualify
1958 did not enter
1962 did not qualify
1966 did not enter
1970 did not qualify
1974 did not qualify
1978 did not qualify
1982 did not qualify
1986 did not qualify
1990 did not qualify
1994 did not qualify

The Coach

Takeshi Okada
Career: played for Furukawa and the national youth and Olympic teams; coached Furukawa and Jef United Ichihara.
Born: August 25, 1956
Appointed: October 1997

Star Performers

Yoshikatsu Kawaguchi
Position: goalkeeper
Club: Yokohama Marinos
Born: August 15, 1975

Masami Ihara
Position: centre back
Club: Yokohama Marinos
Born: September 18, 1967

Hidetoshi Nakata
Position: midfield
Club: Bellmare Hiratsuka
Born: January 22, 1977

Kazuyoshi Miura
Position: forward
Club: Verdy Kawasaki
Born: February 26, 1967

Wagner Lopes
Position: striker
Club: Bellmare Hiratsuka
Born: January 29, 1969

The Road to the Finals

Japan 6–3 Uzbekistan
UAE 0–0 Japan
Japan 1–2 South Korea
Kazakhstan 1–1 Japan
Uzbekistan 1–1 Japan
Japan 1–1 UAE
South Korea 0–2 Japan
Japan 3–0 Kazakhstan
Japan 3–2 Iran*
*Play-off

JAMAICA

Boyz from out of nowhere

Group H

Jamaica are the first country from the English-speaking Caribbean to reach the World Cup finals. To have emerged smiling after one of the longest of campaigns was a triumph not merely of stamina but of spirit and determination to beat the odds.

Jamaica line up before their crucial 1–0 victory over Costa Rica

Jamaica's success has been compared with their 1988 bobsleigh adventure at the Calgary Winter Olympics. But that was a one-off. Jamaica's presence at the World Cup finals is a demonstration of the game's mounting strength in the region – growth which will continue whatever may befall them and their Brazilian coach, Rene Simoes, in France.

Jamaica's success was a shock to those who thought cricket was king in Kingston. But Jack Warner, CONCACAF president, says: "When Jamaica play Trinidad at cricket the crowd is 2,000. When Jamaica play Trinidad at football then it's 25,000. But people abroad don't know that."

They do now – following the qualifying achievement built around the goals of English-based Deon Burton of Derby County. Burton was Jamaica's four-goal top scorer in the final qualifying round and is their most expensive footballer, having cost £1 million when transferred from Portsmouth. Other English-based professionals supporting veterans such as goalkeeper Warren Barrett and defender Durrent Brown include Fitzroy Simpson, Paul Hall and Wimbledon's Robbie Earle.

"We're still only learning," says Simoes. "For us to reach the finals is glorious in itself."

Much has changed

The Jamaican federation was founded in 1910 but did not affiliate to FIFA until 1962 and first entered the World Cup in 1966.

The 1998 campaign began with a 1–0 win away to Surinam. A 2–0 home victory earned progress to a knock-out tie against Barbados and another 3–0 aggregate win. The CONCACAF semi-finals stage comprised three mini-leagues of four nations with the top two qualifying for the final play-off. Jamaica topped their group thanks to a 1–0 win over regional champions Mexico.

So, 10 games played, 10 to go, and it looked long odds against the Jamaicans when they drew 0–0 at home with the US, then crashed 6–0 in Mexico. Worse, they managed only a goalless draw in Canada, and went down 3–1 in Costa Rica. Jamaica won their next three games, all at home, all 1–0. Burton scored the deciders against Canada and Costa Rica, then provided the goal that earned a 1–1 draw in the US.

Suddenly, Jamaica sensed France was a possibility. Burton scored yet again in a 2–2 draw with El Salvador, and a 0–0 draw at home to Mexico made dreams come true for the "Reggae Boyz".

World Cup Record

1930 did not enter
1934 did not enter
1938 did not enter
1950 did not enter
1954 did not enter
1958 did not enter
1962 did not enter
1966 did not qualify
1970 did not qualify
1974 withdrew
1978 did not qualify
1982 did not enter
1986 withdrew
1990 did not qualify
1994 did not qualify

The Coach

Rene Simoes
Career: played for regional lower division clubs in Brazil; coached the Brazilian under-20s, also Rayan SC and Arabi SC (both in Qatar).
Born: March 4, 1953
Appointed: July 1994

Star Performers

Warren Barrett
Position: goalkeeper
Club: Violet Kickers
Born: September 7, 1970

Durrent Brown
Position: central defender
Club: Wadadah
Born: July 8, 1964

Fitzroy Simpson
Position: midfield
Club: Portsmouth (England)
Born: February 26, 1970

Paul Hall
Position: forward
Club: Portsmouth (England)
Born: July 3, 1972

Deon Burton
Position: forward
Club: Derby County (England)
Born: October 25, 1976

The Road to the Finals

Jamaica 0–0 USA
Mexico 6–0 Jamaica
Canada 0–0 Jamaica
Costa Rica 3–1 Jamaica
Jamaica 1–0 El Salvador
Jamaica 1–0 Canada
Jamaica 1–0 Costa Rica
USA 1–1 Jamaica
El Salvador 2–2 Jamaica
Jamaica 0–0 Mexico

CROATIA

A return from disaster

Group H

Croatia's remarkable progress up among the world's top soccer nations began in television studios in Manchester in 1994 when they appeared, for the first time, at the draw of a top-level tournament – the European Championship.

Croatia's players play club football around the world, but have great national pride

Croatia reached the quarter-finals, losing to eventual winners Germany. It was a remarkable feat so soon after the country had emerged from the Yugoslavian civil war. But, for manager Miroslav Blazevic and players such as Zvonimir Boban and Davor Suker, that was just a start. Their "real" target was the World Cup.

The majority of Croatia's players are based with clubs abroad, but that has done nothing to dissipate their national pride. As Suker says: "Everything our country has gone through in the last few years makes us all the more determined to do well. Our people have had little enough to cheer them. We want to give them something of which they can be proud. National pride is worth more to us than to any other team."

Earlier existence

Croatia are not total newcomers. The country existed as an independent entity, albeit under puppet regime conditions, in the 1940s, when Croats organised their own championship and national team. But, under direction from Berlin, they played only other Axis-aligned nations such as Germany, Italy, Bulgaria and Romania.

Croatia remained a significant source of strength and talent within the former Yugoslavia after the war. Dinamo Zagreb – now FC Croatia – and Hajduk Split built impressive records in European club competitions which they have extended since Croatia's independent re-emergence. The first match of the new era was a 2–1 win over the United States on October 17, 1990.

Croatia had clearly come a long way by the time they began their 1998 World Cup campaign. Soon, however, Blazevic was under heavy pressure from critics who suggested that the bubble had burst. Indeed, halfway through the campaign, Denmark were running away with the group, followed by Greece, with Croatia a fragile third.

Thus Suker's goal in Salonika last April may be seen as the most important in the group. He struck 16 minutes from the end, when a draw or defeat would have left Croatia with too much ground to make up. Instead, on the last matchday Croatia won 3–1 in Slovenia to go second and earn a play-off against Ukraine.

Croatia won the first leg in Zagreb by 2–0 but afterwards Ukraine defender Sergei Nahornyak failed a dope test. In Kiev for the second leg, a fumble by goalkeeper Marijan Mrmic cost an early goal and then Croatia had another controversially disallowed. After 27 minutes, however, Boksic lifted Croatia level – and into the World Cup finals.

World Cup Record

This is Croatia's first visit to the World Cup finals

The Coach

Miroslav Blazevic
Career: played for Sarajevo, Rijeka, Sion (Switzerland); coached Sion, Lausanne (Switzerland), Rijeka, Dinamo Zagreb, Grasshopper-Club (Switzerland), Pristina, Dinamo Zagreb, Nantes (France), PAOK Salonika (Greece), FC Croatia Zagreb.
Born: February 10, 1935
Appointed: July 1994

Star Performers

Robert Jarni
Position: full-back
Club: Real Betis (Spain)
Born: October 26, 1968

Zvonimir Boban
Position: midfield
Club: Milan (Italy)
Born: October 8, 1968

Robert Prosinecki
Position: midfield
Club: FC Croatia Zagreb
Born: January 12, 1969

Davor Suker
Position: striker
Club: Real Madrid (Spain)
Born: January 1, 1968

Alen Boksic
Position: forward
Club: Lazio (Italy)
Born: January 31, 1970

The Road to the Finals

Bosnia 1–4 Croatia
Croatia 1–1 Greece
Croatia 1–1 Denmark
Croatia 3–3 Slovenia
Greece 0–1 Croatia
Croatia 3–2 Bosnia
Denmark 3–1 Croatia
Slovenia 1–3 Croatia
Croatia 2–0 Ukraine*
Ukraine 1–1 Croatia*

*Play-offs

THE SUPERSTARS

The Greatest Players

The World Cup is like the night sky – glittering with a thousand stars. All of them bring individual talent and a particular character and personality which, we hope, will light up the World Cup matches that they play in with brilliance and dazzling displays of skill.

The 1998 finals in France offer the usual fascinating guessing game: will the great names live up to their reputations and who will be the comparative unknowns who use the tournament as a stepping stone to glory?

Brazil's Ronaldo and Denilson, Spain's Raùl and Yugoslavia's Predrag Mijatovic are among the new men of whom so much is expected. Stoichkov, Batistuta and Maldini lead the band of superstars who know all about the World Cup challenge and are back for more.

All are united in one ambition: to go for gold. All of them hoping that their names will be sealed up in the World Cup hall of fame.

The Captains Meet: Zinedine Zidane for Europe (left) and Ronaldo for the Rest of the World (right) exchange pleasantries before the exhibition game at the World Cup draw in Marseille in December 1997

FAUSTINO ASPRILLA

Man on a mission

Colombia return to the World Cup finals with an ambition fired by tragic memories of the previous tournament in the United States – none of their stars more determined to succeed at France '98 than Newcastle United's Faustino Asprilla.

"I've never played with anyone quite like Asprilla. He is unique. Some of the skills he shows are something else. He both scores sensational goals himself and creates chances for others"

– Les Ferdinand, Tottenham and England

FAUSTINO ASPRILLA

Position: forward
Club: Newcastle United (England)
Previous clubs: Deportivo Cucuta, Atletico Nacional, Parma (Italy)
Birthdate: November 10, 1969
Birthplace: Tulua
International appearances: 37
International goals: 14

Four years ago Colombia's World Cup dream ended, surprisingly, in the first round and defender Andres Escobar was shot dead on his return home. Initially, few of his team-mates wanted to return to the World Cup stage but, in time, they understood they had a debt to pay and Asprilla's explosive talent is crucial to their effort.

The Newcastle forward can tell a story of rags to riches. One of nine children from the dusty town of Cucuta, he cost Newcastle £6.7 million when then manager Kevin Keegan bought him from Italian club Parma two years ago.

Asprilla was a teenage sensation. By the age of 22 he was Colombia's footballer of the year and starring for Atletico Nacional when he was sold to Parma for what turned out to be a bargain £800,000.

Asprilla's early days in Italy were relatively trouble-free. In three seasons he struck an honourable 23 goals in 78 league games, scored the goals which halted Milan's record 58-game unbeaten run and drew international acclaim in the 1994 World Cup qualifiers. Axed from the national squad on one occasion for breaking curfew, he returned to the fold to score twice in a sensational 5–0 win away to Argentina in Buenos Aires.

By now Asprilla had graduated from being a star footballer to becoming an international personality, complete with paparazzi attention. But the pressure caught up with him. His game suffered. Parma were beaten by Arsenal in the 1994 European Cup-winners Cup Final in Copenhagen. Then Colombia crashed out of the 1994 World Cup finals in the United States amid controversy and tragedy.

On returning home for the New Year holiday in 1995, Asprilla was late back in Italy because of legal and domestic problems. He went on to win the UEFA Cup with Parma but, simultaneously, demanded a transfer after a fall-out with coach Nevio Scala. Ultimately he relented and returned to Parma for pre-season training but soon he was on his way to Newcastle.

Keegan's judgement was questioned long and loud among fans and the media. But Asprilla's talent soon endeared him to the Geordie fans and a hat-trick against Barcelona in the UEFA Champions League at St James' Park last autumn silenced any last doubters.

"If he never kicks another ball for the club, last night's heroics earn him a place alongside Jackie Milburn, Hughie Gallacher and fellow Newcastle immortals," the local newspaper asserted – and that, in the football-mad north-east corner of England, is some praise!

GABRIEL BATISTUTA

Argentine goal machine

Gabriel Batistuta has already hammered out his World Cup warning of what opponents can expect in France this summer – and he did it beneath the gaze of all the rival managers.

GABRIEL BATISTUTA

Position: central striker
Club: Fiorentina (Italy)
Previous clubs: Newell's Old Boys, River Plate, Boca Juniors
Birthdate: February 1, 1969
Birthplace: Avellaneda
International appearances: 54
International goals: 36

"Batistuta shows the same sort of passion for the club which we, the fans, possess"
– Fiorentina fan club leader

Batistuta – nicknamed "Batigol" by his adoring fans at Italy's Fiorentina – smacked two superb goals as the Rest of the World thrashed Europe 5–2 in the all-star match which preceded the finals draw in Marseille last December.

The match subsided in the second half after Batistuta had been substituted but he had done more than enough to send a shiver of anxiety down the spines of potential opponents. He had also done more than enough to convince his own national coach, Daniel Passarella, of his determination to star at France '98.

Passarella had not always been a fan of Batistuta – leaving him out during the qualifying competition. The decision mystified Argentine fans, who recognized their team's need for a brave spearhead in the Batistuta mould. Passarella relented only last autumn. Perhaps he felt that Batistuta needed such a provocation to get the best out of him.

Not that Batistuta's Italian fans need convincing. Batistuta arrived in 1991, having just top-scored with six goals in Argentina's Copa America success. He scored on his home league debut for Fiorentina but the team began the season badly. The turning point came in late November after Batistuta complained in an interview with Italy's biggest-selling sports newspaper that his team-mates were not working as hard as they should for him.

Almost immediately, his goal-scoring prowess returned and within weeks he had scored his first Italian hat-trick. However, it was not enough to prevent the team crashing to the bottom of the league and relegation in 1993.

Not surprisingly, Batistuta found himself in demand but, in response to the fans' pleas, he stayed on to score 16 goals in 26 games and shoot Fiorentina straight back into Serie A at their first attempt. The following season he scored 26 goals (including eight penalties) to become the first Argentine to top the Italian scoring charts since Diego Maradona.

Batistuta's form in his early days in Italy guaranteed a place in the Argentine team. But their second round exit from the 1994 World Cup was the biggest disappointment of "Batigol's" career. He is aware that in the qualifying matches for France '98 Passarella placed more faith in Argentina's new home-grown youngsters than in foreign-based players such as himself, but he is confident of his ability.

"It's natural for a new manager to look at all his options," Batistuta says. "But I can still do a job for him. At 29 I am still in my prime."

DENNIS BERGKAMP

Living up to his name

Dennis Bergkamp is Holland's obvious successor to the attacking command once exerted by Johan Cruyff and then Marco Van Basten. He followed them as the central striker of Ajax and then into the national team. But there the comparisons end for Bergkamp is very much his own man.

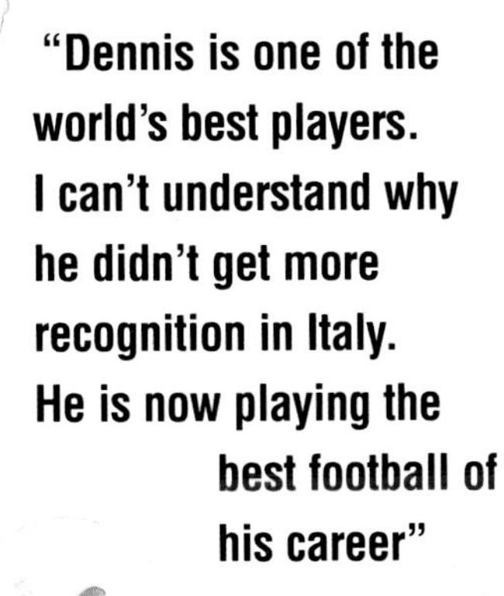

"Dennis is one of the world's best players. I can't understand why he didn't get more recognition in Italy. He is now playing the best football of his career"

– Arsenal coach Arsène Wenger

DENNIS BERGKAMP

Position: forward
Club: Arsenal (England)
Previous clubs: Wilskracht SNL, Ajax, Internazionale (Italy)
Birthdate: May 10, 1969
Birthplace: Amsterdam
International appearances: 55
International goals: 33

Now playing for Arsenal, Bergkamp's destiny was always bound up with great football – right from the day in May 1969 when his family sought to register baby Bergkamp as "Denis" after the father's favourite player, Denis Law.

The registrar refused to accept the name on the grounds that it was too similar to the girl's name Denise. But he compromised to allow "Dennis". Bergkamp's career has hardly suffered.

He made his league debut as a 17-year-old for Ajax against Roda Kerkade in December 1986 and then won a European medal as a substitute when the Dutch giants beat Lokomotiv Leipzig 1–0 in the 1987 European Cup-winners Cup Final in Athens.

Bergkamp's talent was such that Ajax even obtained special dispensation from his school to fly him out on the day of another Cup-winners Cup tie, against Swedish club Malmo, because the match clashed with a school examination.

In 1987–88 Bergkamp scored in 10 consecutive league games, a Dutch record. He and Ajax were well on the way to winning the championship and, in 1990, Bergkamp made his national team debut as a sub against Italy. Two months later, in a match against Greece, Bergkamp scored his first senior level goal for his country.

Bergkamp was voted Dutch Footballer of the Year in 1991 and won another European medal the following year when Ajax beat Torino in the UEFA Cup Final. Unsurprisingly, he attracted the attention of big-money clubs around Europe and soon was on his way to Italy.

His record promised goals aplenty. Some 103 goals in 185 league games for Ajax encouraged the fans of Internazionale to expect great things from the man signed in a joint £12 million deal along with old friend and midfield provider Wim Jonk. Bergkamp did win the UEFA Cup with Inter in 1994, but what the *tifosi* really wanted was the league title and when that proved elusive, Bergkamp moved to Arsenal for £7.5 million.

He adapted quickly to the lifestyle and football in England and, in 1997, signed a new contract which could keep him at Highbury for the rest of his career. Bergkamp formed a fearsome partnership with England striker Ian Wright.

In September 1997, Bergkamp collected a unique honour when three of his more spectacular strikes were selected as the first, second and third best goals in the BBC's Goal of the Month competition.

That's the Bergkamp whom Holland hope to see in the World Cup finals.

JOSE LUIS CHILAVERT

Goalkeeper with a different attitude

***No one in South America was the least surprised when Paraguay's goalkeeper, Jose Luis Felix Chilavert, was proclaimed the continent's 1996 Footballer of the Year in the annual poll run by the Uruguayan newspaper* El Pais.**

JOSE LUIS CHILAVERT

Position: goalkeeper
Club: Velez Sarsfield (Argentina)
Previous clubs: Sportivo Luqueno, San Lorenzo (Argentina), Real Zaragoza (Spain)
Birthdate: July 27, 1965
Birthplace: Luque
International appearances: 54
International goals: 6

"I have broken the mould. In terms of cars some goalkeepers would be Fiats; I would be the latest, most powerful Mercedes Benz"
– Chilavert

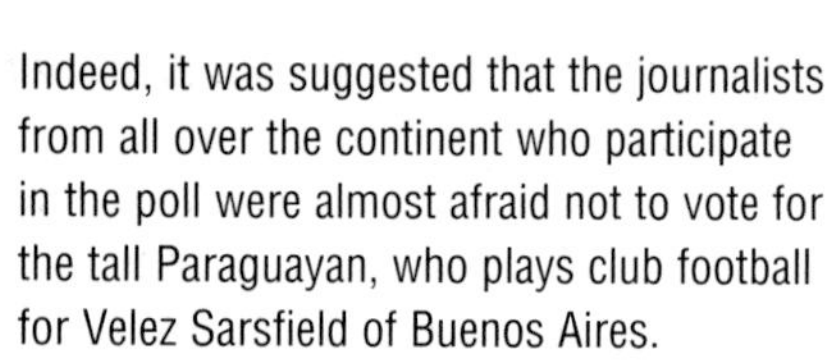

Indeed, it was suggested that the journalists from all over the continent who participate in the poll were almost afraid not to vote for the tall Paraguayan, who plays club football for Velez Sarsfield of Buenos Aires.

Everything about Chilavert's manner is confrontational. On the football field, the snarling bulldog's face, which is on the front of his jersey, seems to say to opposing players, "I dare you to score against me." Off the pitch, one reporter who rashly commented that Chilavert appeared to have put on a few kilos over the close season was sharply smacked around the face for his nerve.

The highest-scoring goalkeeper in the modern history of world football, the Paraguayan was the first goalkeeper ever to finish top of the voting in the 26-year history of South America's top individual football honour.

Chilavert deserves much of the credit for Paraguay's qualification for France '98, not only for the aggressive manner in which he commands his team-mates, and his penalty area, but also for his goals – most notably the free kick which earned a 1–1 draw with Argentina early in the qualifiers.

In front of a hostile 80,000 crowd in the River Plate stadium, having promised at least one goal, Chilavert scored for the 32nd time in his career. It was his second goal of the 1998 World Cup qualifying campaign, having previously converted a penalty against Colombia.

Chilavert's goals have frequently come from expertly-struck free kicks, others from the penalty-spot. Last year Chilavert also achieved a unique double, for a goalkeeper, of scoring against the two greatest club sides in Argentine soccer, River Plate and Boca Juniors.

Further examples of Chilavert's temperament are that he has come to blows on the pitch with team-mates and was once handed a three-month suspended jail sentence after a dispute with a ballboy during a game between Velez Sarsfield and Gimnasia y Esgrima de la Plata in April 1994. He was furious, accusing the Argentine judicial system of exacting revenge on him "because I am Paraguayan and they hate to see a Paraguayan being so successful in their country".

Once the World Cup is over, Chilavert's admirers are confident he will be in demand all over the world.

Many great goalkeepers have found the World Cup finals a daunting stage – from the great Russian Lev Yashin to Colombia's eccentric Rene Higuita. Chilavert sees the tournament merely as the appropriate stage for his genius.

DENILSON

Huge price, huge talent

Denilson will become, after the World Cup, the world's most expensive player. Officials and fans of Betis of Spain expect him to show, in France, why their club have committed £23 million to buying the latest genius to roll off Brazil's football conveyor belt.

"Denilson is so strong physically, and so versatile technically, that he can play equally well in two roles – either as an orthodox attacking midfielder or as a left winger"

– Brazil's national team coach Mario Zagallo

DENILSON

Position: midfielder
Club: São Paulo
Previous club: San Bernardao
Birthdate: August 24, 1977
Birthplace: Didema
International appearances: 14
International goals: 3

National coach Mario Zagallo has few doubts. He believes that the emergence of Denilson de Oliveira can prove the decisive factor in Brazil's bid to win the World Cup for a record fifth time.

French fans have already seen Denilson at work. When he came on in the second half of Brazil's enthralling duel with Italy in the Tournoi de France last summer, his surging runs down the left helped them turn a 3–1 deficit into a 3–3 draw. Then, in the Copa America, Denilson again appeared after half-time to inspire a fightback as Brazil, 2–0 down to Mexico, revived to win 3–2. It proved a turning point as Brazil went on to trounce Peru 7–0 in the semi-final and then overcame hosts Bolivia 3–1 in the Final.

Zagallo was thrilled with his discovery, describing the youngster as two players rolled into one.

"We have always been used to having exceptional wingers with great pace and shooting power, and they have always intimidated our opponents," said Zagallo, a knowledgeable man on the subject having played outside-left in Brazil's World Cup-winning teams in Sweden in 1958 and in Chile in 1962.

"I thought they had disappeared from our game. It's great for football to have a player like this re-emerge."

Denilson made his name when with a youth team named San Bernardao and came to the attention of São Paulo FC – the top club in his home city – when he inspired a 7–0 thrashing of the local giants in a youth tournament. After the match he was sold to São Paulo, with whom he first earned headlines as the result of a brilliant individual goal in a South American CONMEBOL Cup match.

A year later Denilson had forced his way into Brazil's youth team, who finished runners-up to Argentina in the 1995 World Youth Cup. Little more than a year later, in November 1996, he was handed his national team debut in a 2–0 win over Cameroon in a friendly. Then came his match-saving performances in the Tournoi de France and Copa America. Denilson continued to display good form in the Confederation Cup in Saudi Arabia at the end of 1997, scoring again in the 3–0 destruction of Mexico.

"He's still a young player and he mustn't get carried away with all the praise that is being heaped on him," said Zagallo. "He keeps the ball to himself too much sometimes. But it's a small fault – and he's still only a youngster."

And that's exactly what will frighten Brazil's opponents.

YOURI DJORKAEFF

Defending the family honour

Youri Djorkaeff has family honour to defend at the World Cup – father Jean having been a key figure at full-back for France at the finals in England in 1966. But not for Youri the satisfaction of sealing gaps, covering team-mates and denying forwards time and space.

YOURI DJORKAEFF

Position: midfielder
Club: Internazionale (Italy)
Previous clubs: Grenoble, Strasbourg, Monaco, Paris Saint-Germain
Birthdate: March 9, 1968
Birthplace: Lyon
International appearances: 31
International goals: 17

"At his best, Youri Djorkaeff is two men. He is an attacker and, simultaneously, he is also working as a midfielder"

– France national team coach Aimé Jacquet

Youri is not a defender but an attacking midfielder – and such an effective one that he has been one of the brightest stars in Italy's Serie A since joining Internazionale of Milan two years ago.

Djorkaeff has succeeded Eric Cantona and David Ginola as one of the No. 1 pin-ups of French fans. They admire and respect the achievements of Didier Deschamps at Juventus but Djorkaeff provides the heady mixture of excitement and unpredictable flair which brings crowds to their feet.

It took him only four weeks to find a place in the hearts of Inter's demanding fans when he scored with a spectacular bicycle-kick against Atalanta. Djorkaeff's vision and drive guided Inter through to the UEFA Cup Final, then helped convert them into league contenders once more after years in the shadow of city rivals Milan.

Djorkaeff began his career in professional football with Grenoble, made his name with Monaco – with whom he was the league's leading scorer in 1993–94 – and then emerged as international class after inspiring Paris Saint-Germain to their 1996 European Cup-winners Cup triumph. Both for club and country he used his mobility and football intellect to establish himself in a wandering role somewhere between the strikers and midfield.

Djorkaeff was handed a painful France debut in the autumn of 1993, appearing as a substitute against Israel in the 1994 World Cup qualifiers. A win would have taken France to the finals but instead they went down 3–2. Djorkaeff was axed until the following spring.

Then the player scored the only goal in a victory over Italy in Naples. It was a hugely significant strike. Not only did it establish Djorkaeff as a new French footballing hero, but it also brought his talents to the attention of a considerable Italian audience.

He scored in his next match against Chile and then again against Japan to make it three goals in three games. Always a man for the vital goal, it was Djorkaeff whose vital equaliser against Poland in the last Euro 96 qualifying match – a result which took the French through to the final tournament – probably kept manager Aimé Jacquet in his job.

France went on to reach the semi-finals at that European Championship. Djorkaeff and Jacquet were both disappointed not to go further. But, as Djorkaeff said after the shoot-out defeat by the Czech Republic: "We came so very close. But in the World Cup, remember, we shall have an extra player – our fans."

GHEORGHE HAGI

Glorious swansong

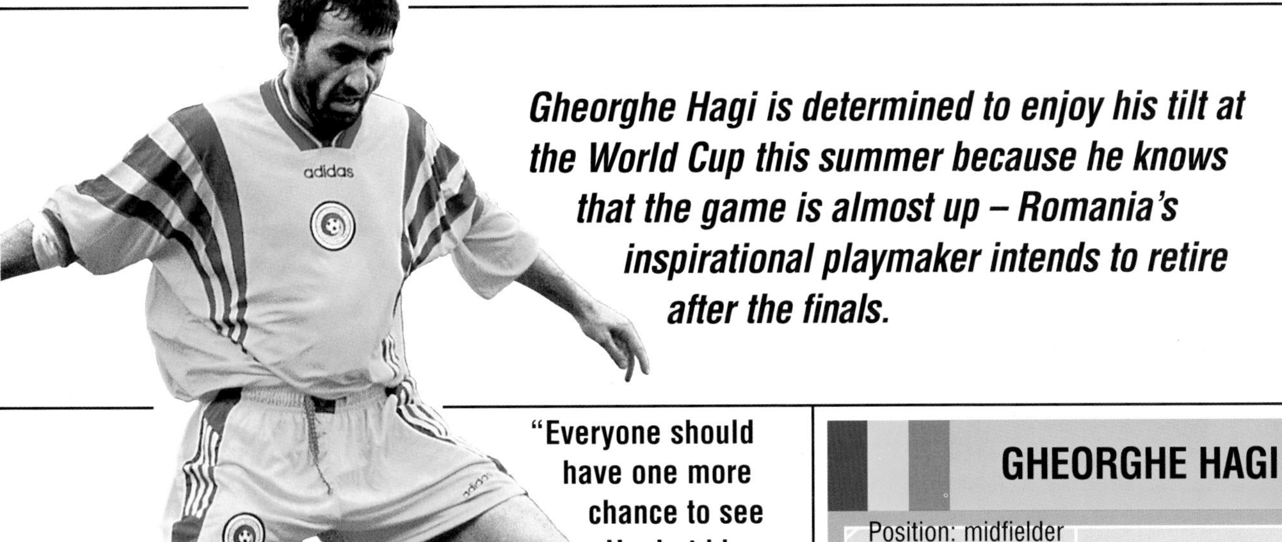

Gheorghe Hagi is determined to enjoy his tilt at the World Cup this summer because he knows that the game is almost up – Romania's inspirational playmaker intends to retire after the finals.

"Everyone should have one more chance to see Hagi at his best"

– Former Romania coach Lucescu

GHEORGHE HAGI

Position: midfielder
Club: Galatasaray (Turkey)
Previous clubs: Constanta, Sportul Studentesc, Steaua Bucharest, Real Madrid (Spain), Brescia (Italy), Barcelona (Spain)
Birthdate: February 5, 1965
Birthplace: Sacele
International appearances: 107
International goals: 32

Hagi will be appearing at his third successive World Cup and hoping for a little more luck. He was midfield general in the sides which both fell in penalty shoot-outs, to the Republic of Ireland in the second round in 1990 and then to Sweden in the quarter-finals at USA '94.

Romania and Hagi suffered a depressing time of it at the 1996 European Championship finals when Romania finished bottom of their group after having a perfectly good "goal" disallowed because the ball ricocheted back into play too fast for referee Peter Mikkelsen to see. Now the old guard have the chance of one last hurrah.

Scotland manager Craig Brown considered Romania the best team in the European qualifying section and Hagi was the key to everything. He may have stepped aside from the top-level continental club mainstream – Galatasaray lacking the profile of a Real Madrid or Barcelona – but Hagi remains one of the most artistic influences around.

Hagi's talent was first the subject of covetous attentions one month before his 23rd birthday in 1988, when the son of ruthless dictator Nicolae Ceaucescu forced Sportul Studentesc to "give" Hagi to the army club and then European champions, Steaua Bucharest.

In nearly four seasons at Steaua the owner of one of the world's most mercurial left feet scored 76 goals in 97 league games. This attracted Real Madrid but, while the Spanish fans liked Hagi, his team-mates grumbled about having to fetch and carry for him in midfield so he was sold to Italian club Brescia.

It was the nearest thing to a move back to his home country since Mircea Lucescu, a former Romanian national coach, was the Brescia boss and three fellow internationals played there – Dorin Mateut, Ioan Sabau and Florin Raducioiu.

Hagi duly starred at the World Cup in the United States before returning to Spain. New club Barcelona, however, had no more intention than Real Madrid of bending their team strategy to suit Hagi's needs. He spent more and more time on the subs' bench before transferring to Galatasaray.

To his Romanian admirers, however, Hagi remains supreme. Thousands turned out for his wedding back in his home town of Constanta and it was headline news when he funded a western-style, fully-equipped dental surgery in Bucharest.

But, like so many players who love the game more than its rewards, Hagi can think of nothing more important now than his last World Cup.

JURGEN KLINSMANN

European traveller

Jürgen Klinsmann reached a century of international appearances for Germany last autumn with everything to prove after having gone a remarkable 854 minutes – the equivalent of nine and a half games – without a goal for his country.

JURGEN KLINSMANN

Position: striker
Club: Tottenham Hotspur (England)
Previous clubs: Stuttgarter Kickers, Stuttgart, Inter (Italy), Monaco (France), Tottenham (England), Bayern Munich, Sampdoria (Italy)
Birthdate: July 30, 1964
Birthplace: Goppingen
International appearances: 100
International goals: 43

"Jürgen is an ideal captain because a successful team needs a leader"
– Franz Beckenbauer

Then, just when his fellow countrymen were starting to wonder if the baker's son had lost the penalty box yeast, "Klinsi" hit back with two goals in a 4–0 win over Armenia which shot Germany closer to the World Cup finals in France.

Klinsmann took it all in his stride, saying: "I had no doubts about my ability. I had just been unlucky. It's normal. It happens to strikers. We have to live with it."

Klinsmann carries extra responsibility as captain of Germany – his experience being second to none, after a career which has taken him on a European club odyssey from Germany to Italy to France to England, back to Germany and then back once more to Italy and then England again.

Klinsmann, who has resisted the move back into midfield beloved of many an ageing striker, was seen at his World Cup best when he helped West Germany win the 1990 tournament in Italy. His inspirational display in the second round victory over Holland was probably the greatest single performance of his career.

After the finals he stayed in Italy, joining World Cup-winning team-mates Lothar Matthäus and Andy Brehme at Internazionale of Milan, with whom he won the UEFA Cup the following season. This was followed by a move to France and Monaco, with whom he appeared in the Champions League.

Klinsmann's next move was to England and his subsequent success at Tottenham Hotspur meant that his name was linked with almost every top-level coaching vacancy in the English game. Nevertheless, it's by no means certain a man with wide-ranging interests beyond football would want to stay in the game after his retirement.

After a year in England, it was back home to Bayern Munich, where Klinsmann collected a German championship title in 1997. This was followed by a second spell in Italy, this time with Sampdoria, before he rejoined a struggling Tottenham side last December.

Before Klinsmann, only two other German players had reached a century of international appearances: Matthäus with 122 and Franz Beckenbauer with 103. "Klinsi" has already emulated them in that sphere. Now he may match their other claim to fame as World Cup-winning captains.

Klinsmann already knows the joy of lifting a major international trophy, having captained Germany to victory at the 1996 European Championship. Now, with national team retirement imminent, he knows that this is his last chance to go one better.

ALEXI LALAS

A cool dude

The United States will be looking to the experience of guitar-strumming Alexi Lalas, the first American to have played in Italy's Serie A, to command their World Cup defence once more.

"We have had more interest in Alexi from foreign clubs than any other player we have ever had. It's not even close"
– USSF official Sunil Gulati

ALEXI LALAS

Position: central defender
Club: New England Revolution
Previous clubs: Rutgers University, Padova (Italy)
Birthdate: June 1, 1970
Birthplace: Birmingham, Michigan
International appearances: 91
International goals: 9

But Lalas – who describes himself as a "dude from Detroit" – is in fact equally at home in the clubs and bars where he has regularly performed with his own rock band as out on the soccer pitches of the world performing with club and country.

Lalas, who became a hero in the United States when his goal helped beat England 2–0 in a 1993 friendly in Boston, grew up playing ice hockey in Detroit. But he turned his back on a promising career in that sport in favour of pursuing his interest in soccer. He describes the goal against England in that friendly as the turning point of his career – "It boosted my confidence and extended my run in the team."

Lalas, of the flowing red hair and goatee beard, became the symbol of American soccer after the hosts reached the second round during their successful 1994 World Cup campaign. Within weeks he had been snapped up by Italian provincial club Padova, who had just won promotion to Serie A. Lalas had never played in a professional championship. But, caricatured in various guises from Buffalo Bill to General Custer and Uncle Sam, he soon achieved heroic status in the ancient university town of Padua.

In the 1994–95 season, Padova and Lalas struggled to avoid relegation and stayed up only thanks to a penalty shoot-out win after a play-off with Genoa. Nevertheless, despite his club's poor showing Lalas was rated by some Italian reporters up alongside Brazil's Aldair, Gianluca Vialli of Juventus and Argentina's Gabriel Batistuta as one of the best players of the season.

Padova were, in fact, relegated the next season but by then Lalas had returned home to the United States to join the Major League Soccer adventure. Looking back, Lalas believes the game is taken too seriously in Italy. He says: "It's wonderful to play soccer, but if you don't have a life off the pitch you go crazy."

The US 1991 College Player of the Year adds: "All through my career I have been told I don't deserve to be where I am. First they said I shouldn't be in the 1992 Olympic team, then the 1994 World Cup squad. But I know I have done my best at the very summit of the game. I believe it's always better to have tried and failed rather than not to have tried at all."

Lalas was once asked what his reaction would be if both a record company and a soccer club made simultaneous job offers.

Unhesitatingly, he told the reporter: "I'm going to strum my guitar. I can be 99 years old and still hook up the guitar but I can't run for ever."

MICHAEL LAUDRUP

Have boots, will travel

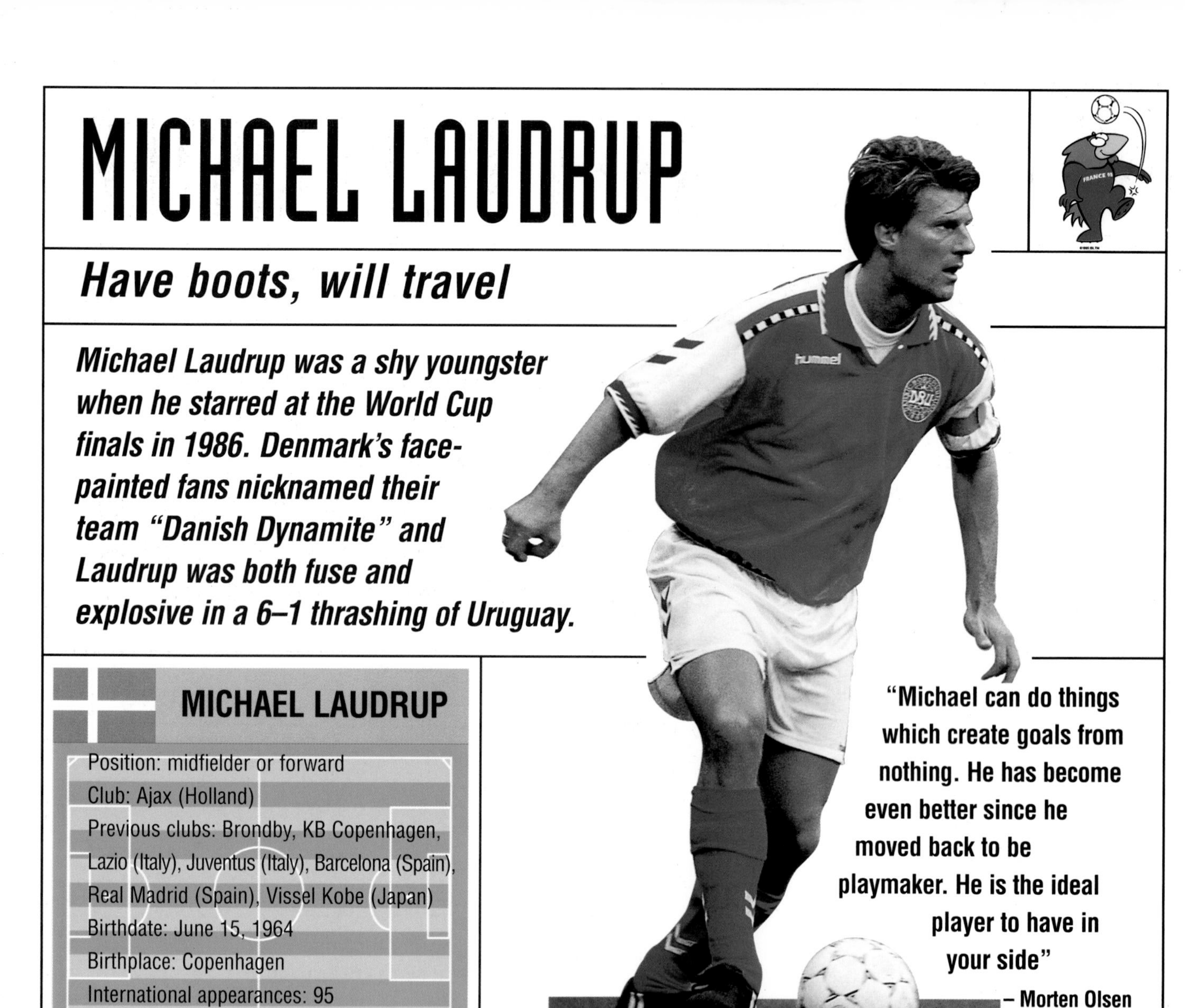

Michael Laudrup was a shy youngster when he starred at the World Cup finals in 1986. Denmark's face-painted fans nicknamed their team "Danish Dynamite" and Laudrup was both fuse and explosive in a 6–1 thrashing of Uruguay.

MICHAEL LAUDRUP

Position: midfielder or forward
Club: Ajax (Holland)
Previous clubs: Brondby, KB Copenhagen, Lazio (Italy), Juventus (Italy), Barcelona (Spain), Real Madrid (Spain), Vissel Kobe (Japan)
Birthdate: June 15, 1964
Birthplace: Copenhagen
International appearances: 95
International goals: 36

"Michael can do things which create goals from nothing. He has become even better since he moved back to be playmaker. He is the ideal player to have in your side"

– Morten Olsen

"This is a player we had never heard of before," said Uruguayan defender Nelson Gutierrez. "But why not? He must be the greatest footballer in the world."

No one has been left in ignorance since by a brilliant career which has taken Laudrup to some of the world's top clubs – Lazio and Juventus in Italy, Barcelona and Real Madrid in Spain, then Holland's Ajax with a brief intermission helping establish soccer in Japan with Vissel Kobe.

Clearly Laudrup, possibly Denmark's finest product, has felt the provocation of a new challenge essential every few years to re-ignite the talent which made him the most coveted teenager in Europe. Now he may be the most coveted veteran.

Michael – the elder brother of Brian – played first in the boys section of the Vanlose club in Copenhagen at which his father Finn Laudrup – himself a former Danish international – had begun. At 14 Michael joined the youth section of the Brondbyernes club before moving to KB Copenhagen. Laudrup made his league debut for KB at 17 against Aarhus, then returned to Brondby under the tutelage of his father.

Soon the phone began to ring with calls from scouts and clubs. In the end the Laudrups opted for Juventus – who lent Laudrup to Lazio initially before recalling him in time to help them win the 1985 World Club Cup. A year later Laudrup was starring on a world stage again – this time at the 1986 World Cup.

Back in Europe, Laudrup grew increasingly discontented with Italian football and moved on to Barcelona with whom he won both the European Champions and Cup-winners Cup as well as four Spanish league titles under Johan Cruyff. Eventually, Laudrup and Cruyff fell out. The last straw for Laudrup was being omitted from Barcelona's team for the 1994 Champions Cup Final against Milan. Within weeks he had joined Real Madrid.

Cruyff was not the only coach with whom Laudrup fell out. Disagreements with Denmark boss Richard Moller Nielsen meant Laudrup missed the national team's shock win at the 1992 European Championship.

The two men made their peace afterward but Denmark failed to qualify for the 1994 World Cup finals and fell in the first round of Euro 96.

That was when Laudrup answered the call of Japan's J.League and Europe thought it had seen the last of the Dane. But 12 years after first lighting up the World Cup Finals, Michael Laudrup is back where he belongs.

GARY McALLISTER

A man to depend on

Gary McAllister knows all about the weight of leadership and experience. He was the man entrusted with a potentially vital penalty for Scotland against hosts England in the finals of the European Championship two years ago – and who saw his kick saved by keeper David Seaman.

"Gary gets as much out of himself as he possibly can. In football terms, he's never been happy to stay just as he is"
– Former national and club team-mate Gordon Strachan

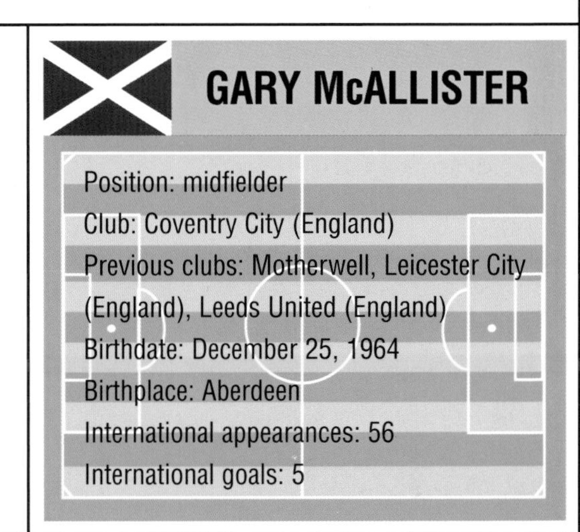

GARY McALLISTER

Position: midfielder
Club: Coventry City (England)
Previous clubs: Motherwell, Leicester City (England), Leeds United (England)
Birthdate: December 25, 1964
Birthplace: Aberdeen
International appearances: 56
International goals: 5

Coventry's 33-year-old midfield general admitted that the Euro 96 incident left him low. "It's not one of those career moments I like to recall," McAllister said. He has more than made amends by guiding Scotland through to their sixth finals appearance in the last seven World Cups.

McAllister's potential had not been immediately obvious as a teenager with struggling Motherwell. But manager Tommy McLean compared the young McAllister with Liverpool iron man Graeme Souness in terms of vision of play and quality of passing. Leicester City thought the same and they paid a mere £150,000 to sign McAllister in 1985. Under the astute guidance of manager David Pleat – one of England's more innovative coaches – his game developed by leaps and bounds.

Nottingham Forest tried to sign him in 1990, but the deal went wrong after McAllister met with eccentric manager Brian Clough. Instead, he joined Leeds United for £1 million and, two years later, was celebrating league championship success.

It was under the managership of Howard Wilkinson that McAllister honed his leadership skills since the captain at Leeds must do much more than toss up before a match. Thus McAllister found himself acting as a go-between for manager and squad as well as helping organize the rota for charity, social and sponsorship activities.

Setbacks have been few and far between but all of them have been outweighed by the honour of captaining his country.

Two years ago – in the wake of his generally excellent Euro 96 performances – McAllister was coveted by a string of top clubs including Scottish champions Rangers. But he surprised his many admirers by transferring to unfashionable Coventry City, where old Leeds colleague Gordon Strachan was now player-manager.

It made no difference to his security of tenure in Scotland's midfield. McAllister had made his debut in inauspicious circumstances, a 1–0 home defeat by East Germany, in April 1990. His thoughtful style, unerringly accurate passing and self-control made him not merely an automatic choice but obvious captaincy material.

The penalty miss against England at Euro 96 remains merely one of those twists of fate which befall every player from time to time. It has not disturbed McAllister's confidence or the respect in which his managers and team-mates hold him.

McAllister remains a typical new age sportsman, a sort of executive footballer. As Scotland manager Craig Brown once said: "You can almost imagine him having a mobile phone out on the pitch."

PAOLO MALDINI

Like father, like son

Skipper Paolo Maldini goes into the 1998 World Cup finals heading toward a century of international appearances and, beyond that, the prospect of becoming Italy's most-capped international of all time.

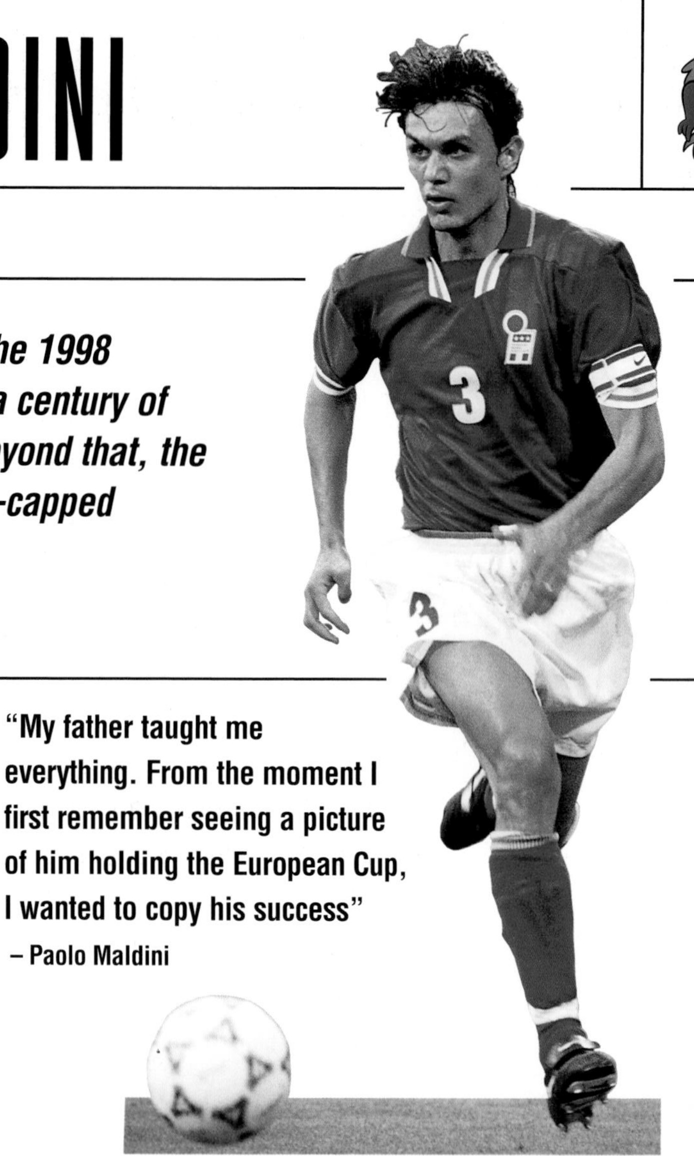

"My father taught me everything. From the moment I first remember seeing a picture of him holding the European Cup, I wanted to copy his success"
– Paolo Maldini

He owes much of his success to the national team's coach – his father, Cesare Maldini, himself captain of Milan's first European Champions Cup-winning team back in 1963.

Left-back Paolo duly followed in father's Europe-conquering footsteps in three memorable Finals: against Steaua Bucharest in Barcelona in 1989, Benfica in Vienna in 1990 and Barcelona in Athens in 1994. But Maldini junior insists there have been no favours along the way.

If anything his father, when Milan youth coach, worked Paolo harder than the rest of the Milan youngsters before being lured away to join the coaching staff of the Italian federation.

"I think my father was harder on me because he didn't want any one to accuse him of favouritism," says Paolo. "In the long run that made me try harder to succeed. I wanted to do it for myself, but I owe it to him."

Paolo is taller, leaner and quicker than his father was, and his reading of a game – once considered a weakness – is now quite as astute. At World Cup level he has surpassed his father's achievements after collecting a runners-up medal in the dramatic penalty shoot-out defeat by Brazil in Pasadena in 1994.

Maldini's form suffered afterward through fatigue, niggling injuries and as a consequence of problems within Milan. But his record leaves no doubt as to the natural talent of a worthy successor to great Italian defenders such as Giacinto Facchetti.

Maldini made his Milan debut away to Udinese in January 1985, at the age of 16, and his senior Italy debut as a substitute in a goalless draw against Yugoslavia in March 1988. Three months later he was starring for Italy at the European Championship in West Germany.

Italy fell in the semi-finals at that tournament to the Soviet Union. But it was obvious that a fine team was being created and that Maldini would be a fixture on the international scene for more than a decade to come – barring accidents.

Media recognition arrived with an award as World Player of the Year in 1994 from the London magazine *World Soccer*. Maldini was thrilled, saying: "That was a great honour for me because defenders, generally, receive so much less attention from fans and media than goalscorers. We are more in the engine room rather than taking the glory."

The glory was tinged with regret after that World Cup "failure" four years ago. That's why Maldini intends going just one step further, in France.

PREDRAG MIJATOVIC

Unknown superstar

When Ronaldo was asked to name the handful of players who might be his rivals as outstanding individual at the 1998 World Cup finals he took no time over the first name: Predrag "Predja" Mijatovic of Yugoslavia.

"I am very ambitious and very serious about my football and I want to reach the very top. That is why I came to play in western Europe – and that's why the World Cup means so much to me"
– Mijatovic

PREDRAG MIJATOVIC

Position: forward
Club: Real Madrid (Spain)
Previous clubs: Buducnost Titograd, Partizan Belgrade, Valencia (Spain)
Birthdate: January 19, 1969
Birthplace: Podgorica
International appearances: 26
International goals: 14

The Real Madrid man might not be the most famous striker in Europe. At Madrid he may even be considered as in the shadow of Spain's Raul and Croatia's Davor Suker. But his top-scoring 14-goal performance for Yugoslavia in the World Cup qualifiers marked him out as a striker to fear.

As Ronaldo, who moved from Barcelona to Internazionale last summer, said: "One of the great reliefs about leaving Spanish football was knowing I would not have to play against a team with Mijatovic in it. Most people don't realize just how good he is."

Born in the Yugoslav republic of Montenegro – the same republic which produced Milan's star midfielder Dejan Savicevic – Mijatovic comes from a middle class background. His father was a doctor who dabbled in photography. Thus Mijatovic's childhood albums are packed with pictures of him playing football and, even better, scoring goals.

His penalty-box talents were noted by local league club Buducnost Titograd. He was in the first team at 17. Then came a transfer to the army club, Partizan Belgrade, where Mijatovic quickly established himself as the top home-based star. Not that the rest of Europe knew. War in the Balkans brought international suspension for both the national team and the top clubs.

Valencia "rescued" Mijatovic from talented, frustrated anonymity. He spent three years with the Spanish club. But, while building a reputation as a "Slav Hugo Sanchez" – for the danger he creates inside a penalty box – he won nothing and began to grow impatient. His agent contacted Barcelona. But then coach Johan Cruyff was not impressed.

So Mijatovic waited a further year, until the summer of 1996, then signed for Real Madrid for £3 million. Fans appreciated the player but wondered how he would settle in alongside the other new arrival, centre-forward Davor Suker who, as a Croat, came from the other side of the warring Balkan divide.

"No problem," says Mijatovic. "All of us Serbs, Montenegrins, Croats, Slovenes and Bosnians in Spanish football get on well. We appreciate each other as human beings and footballers and that's enough."

No one can doubt Mijatovic's gift for goals. He was the top scorer in the World Cup's European qualifying section – including four in the 7–1 play-off thrashing of Hungary in Budapest. Only seven other players worldwide reached double figures in the various qualifying competitions for the 1998 World Cup – and most of those played many more games.

RONALDO

Brightest of stars

Ronaldo is the world's No. 1 footballer – as decided by FIFA two years in a row. Still only 21, he has already achieved his destiny after having developed into the world's most expensive player.

RONALDO

Position: central striker
Club: Internazionale (Italy)
Previous clubs: Cruzeiro, PSV Eindhoven (Holland), Barcelona (Spain)
Birthdate: September 22, 1976
Birthplace: Belo Horizonte
International appearances: 29
International goals: 20

"Go anywhere in the world and you won't find another player who can score goals like Ronaldo. He's simply sensational"
– Former Barcelona and England national coach Bobby Robson

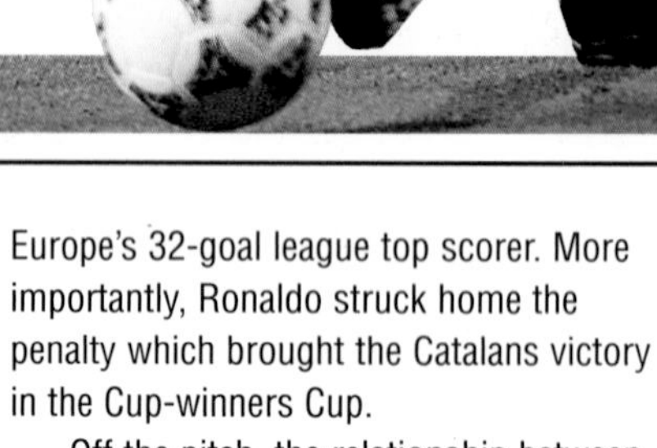

Dutch club PSV Eindhoven brought him to Europe but he was always destined for the bright lights and hothouse atmosphere of Italy or Spain.

The questions were: when and to whom? At first Italy's Internazionale headed the queue after Ronaldo spent a week in Milan as their guest in the summer of 1995. Inter even paid PSV for first option should the Dutch club decide to sell – which they did in 1996.

Ronaldo's potential earned him a place in Brazil's 1994 World Cup-winning squad in the United States. It was national team coach Mario Zagallo who wanted to include him just so that he could get experience on the big stage.

It says everything for Ronaldo's power and skill that potential purchasers were not put off by the knee trouble which kept the striker out of action for most of the second half of the 1995–96 season. Surgery and rest were prescribed so that Ronaldo could be fit to play for Brazil at the Olympic Games finals in Atlanta. At the Games, Brazil – hot favourites to win the gold medal – reached the semi-finals before falling, in a most dramatic finale, to the ultimate champions, Nigeria.

In the meantime Inter and Barcelona had entered into an auction over the price of Ronaldo's transfer fee. The Catalan giants agreed to meet PSV's valuation of £12.5 million while the Italians, given the chance to compete, pulled back. Barcelona moved quickly to negotiate a six-year contract which earned Ronaldo around £8 million before bonuses.

Barcelona had no doubt that he was worth the money and he proved the point in 1996–97, the only season he spent with the club, by winning the Golden Boot as Europe's 32-goal league top scorer. More importantly, Ronaldo struck home the penalty which brought the Catalans victory in the Cup-winners Cup.

Off the pitch, the relationship between Ronaldo and Barcelona turned sour and he eventually bought out his contract, with FIFA forced to step in to make a judgement on the fee. They decided that Ronaldo could move to Inter and set the transfer price at a world record £19.5 million.

He has already been voted FIFA's World Footballer of the Year twice in a row (the first time someone has picked up the award back-to-back) and the awards keep piling up. Ronaldo has one World Cup-winner's medal, as a non-playing member of Brazil's squad in 1994. He was taken along to that tournament only for the ride, to gain experience. Now, in France, Brazil expect him to be the star of the show.

MARCELO SALAS

Hitting the bull's-eye

Chilean striker Marcelo Salas is the new superstar of South American football – especially since his hat-trick inspired a 4–0 World Cup qualifying victory over Peru which put his home country on the road to France.

"Although money is important, I'm not interested in playing for a team who will pay me a lot but have no chance of winning prizes. I love the glory!"
– Salas

MARCELO SALAS

Position: central striker
Club: River Plate (Argentina)
Previous clubs: Santos Temuco, Universidad de Chile
Birthdate: December 24, 1974
Birthplace: Temuco
International appearances: 31
International goals: 21

Salas, 23 and nicknamed El Matador, made his name with Universidad de Chile, then River Plate of Argentina, whom he joined for £2.2 million in the summer of 1996. Within a year of moving to the Buenos Aires side he became the subject of £10+ million enquiries from major clubs in England, Italy and Spain.

Salas learned his football amid concrete wasteland and rubble in the working class suburb of Nahuelbuta in Temuco. One childhood friend recalled: "Marcelo was always there two hours before the rest of us, playing with the ball, practising free kicks. He always knew he was going to make the big-time."

Marcelo's father, Rosember, pleaded with Deportivo Temuco to give his son a contract. It was not as if he was asking big money – just enough to pay for the boy's tracksuit and boots. But the club were not impressed by what they saw and nobody even turned up at a meeting Rosember had arranged.

Santos, Deportivo's even poorer city rivals, had more sense and did at least give Salas a chance, but took it no further. Salas's favourite team, Colo Colo from the capital Santiago, also rejected the chance to take Salas on trial. So, at 16 years old, he joined Santiago rivals Universidad de Chile. At 19 he was in the first team and scoring the goals with which "U" won two successive league titles.

By that time Salas had already been called up for the national squad, having been included in 1994, and he was the youngest Chilean player on show at the 1995 Copa America. Within another year Salas had been sold to River Plate and his goals brought them two Argentine league titles to add to his double in Chile.

By now his fame had spread beyond South America, thanks to his goals in the World Cup qualifiers. Salas claimed 11 of Chile's 32 goals – the largest country total in the South American section – and his partnership with Ivan Zamorano proved one of the most prolific in the qualifiers.

Salas marked his promotion to captain in the penultimate tie against Peru with a hat-trick. He had been handed the armband at his own request after injuries and suspensions to more senior players. National coach Nelson Acosta told him before the game: "If you score two goals, you can be captain again for our last match, against Bolivia."

Chile duly won that one too, by 3–0. Salas scored Chile's second goal and there was no prouder player on the pitch. In little more than six years, he had gone from outcast to superstar.

MATTHIAS SAMMER

Going for a hat-trick

Matthias Sammer became the first East German international to carry off the treasured Golden Ball award as European Footballer of the Year in December 1996. Now he dreams of becoming the first ex-East German to carry off the World Cup.

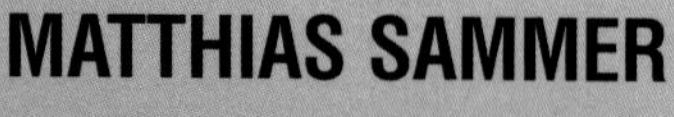

MATTHIAS SAMMER

Position: sweeper
Club: Borussia Dortmund
Previous clubs: Groditz, Einheit Dresden, Dynamo Dresden, Stuttgart, Inter (Italy)
Birthdate: September 5, 1967
Birthplace: Dresden
International appearances: 51 (23 for East Germany)
International goals: 8 (6 for East Germany)

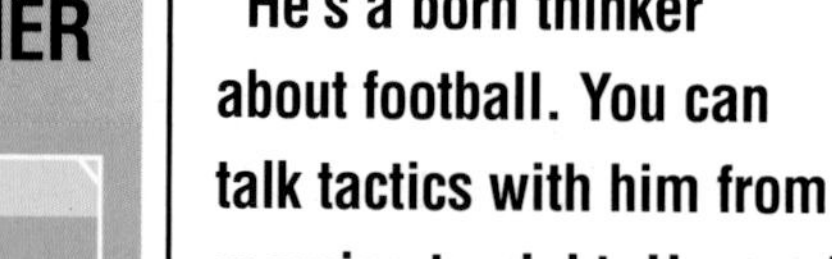

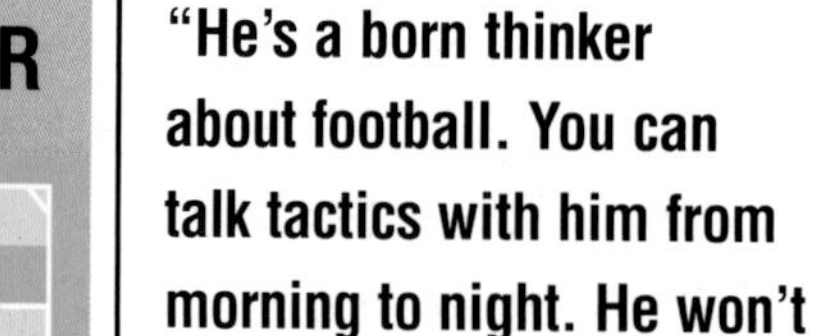

"He's a born thinker about football. You can talk tactics with him from morning to night. He won't need to study to be a coach – he's graduated already!"

– National coach Berti Vogts

German fans worry more about Sammer's fitness than their national team's prospects of winning in France. The Germans boast a fabulous World Cup record. But their prospects of extending or even improving it rest heavily on the wiry shoulders of the attacking sweeper from Borussia Dortmund.

And injury cost Sammer most of the first half of the 1997–98 season after he had tasted Cup-winning glory when he helped inspire Dortmund's victory over Juventus of Italy in the 1997 UEFA Champions League Final in Munich.

Sammer is the nearest thing Germany have had to a successor to Franz Beckenbauer – a defender who appears equally at home when he strides up into midfield. That is hardly surprising since midfield is where Sammer played early on in his career and where his father won caps for the old East Germany.

Klaus Sammer had been a midfield general with Dresden and East Germany. He had barely retired before son Matthias was making his own reputation. In 1986 Sammer guided East Germany to the European youth title. He was promoted immediately into the senior squad, helping Dresden win the league in 1989 and the league and cup double a year later.

The summer of 1990 also brought the collapse of the Berlin Wall – and Sammer was immediately brought to the West by Stuttgart. It was in his new home of the Neckarstadion that he became, the following December, the first East German to play for unified Germany in a 4–0 defeat of Switzerland.

Sammer held his place for a season then displeased national boss Berti Vogts by pulling out of a friendly against England on the grounds of injury, but played in the Bundesliga the next weekend. He was dropped and was not recalled until the 1992 European Championship.

Sweden was not a happy memory. Sammer lacked even a spark of form in the shock Final defeat by Denmark and was replaced at half-time. It was the start of a dismal nine months.

Internazionale had already agreed to buy Sammer from Stuttgart but he never came to grips with the lifestyle or football in Italy and Dortmund brought him home after only six months. The fee, a German record of £4 million, was ridiculed as way over the top for a midfielder-cum-sweeper. But when Sammer, pulling the strings from the heart of defence, masterminded Dortmund's 1995 league title success, the laughing stopped.

First came Euro '96, 1997 brought the Champions League triumph. Will Sammer make it three out of three in 1998?

ALAN SHEARER

Leading from the front

Alan Shearer fulfilled one ambition when a world record £15 million transfer took him home to Newcastle United, whom he had supported as a boy, in July 1996.

"When it comes to putting the ball in the back of the net Alan is the best. I'm glad we've got him on our side!"
– Glenn Hoddle

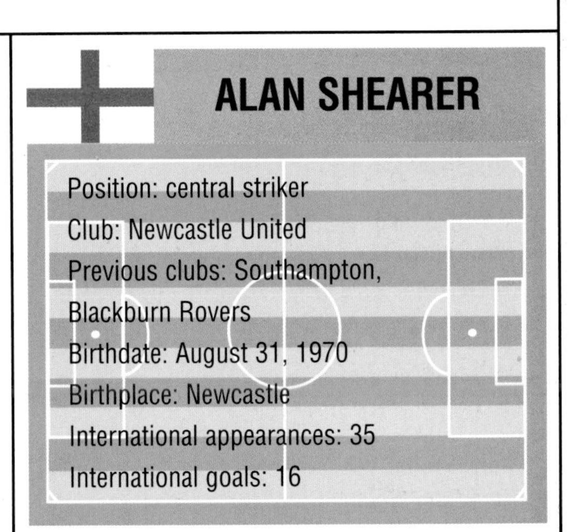

Shearer, who was brought up in nearby Gosforth, had always dreamed that one day he would wear the black and white stripes. Not only, however, was that his dream – he also believed it to be his destiny. As he once said: "I don't know what I'd have done if I hadn't become a footballer. There was nothing else I was interested in doing."

At 14 Shearer got his first chance. Buoyed by having netted 13 goals in one match for his school team a few weeks previously, he arrived at the club of his dreams for trials – and was turned down.

Newcastle's loss was Southampton's gain. The south coast club had a scout in the northeast of England who recognized Shearer's talent and persuaded him to sign. Shearer says: "I had to leave my friends and family, and I was only 16. But if you want to be a professional footballer those are the sacrifices you have to make."

The 17-year-old announced his arrival with a hat-trick against Arsenal, the youngest player to score three in one game in England's top division. Shearer scored 13 goals in 11 matches for England's under-21s and snatched two more against France at Wembley when he eventually earned promotion – under Graham Taylor – to the senior team.

In 1992 Blackburn Rovers, busy buying themselves a side capable of winning the championship, signed Shearer for a British record fee of £3.3 million. He repaid the fee by scoring more than 120 goals in four years – and despite missing half of one season because of a knee injury. He scored 34 goals in each of two consecutive seasons and thus inspired Blackburn to their first title in 81 years.

But the player who could not stop scoring in the Premier League ran into an international dead-end. In the run-up to Euro 96 Shearer went 10 successive games without scoring – a record for an England centre-forward.

Finally the floodgates opened when Shearer scored England's goal in their 1–1 draw with Switzerland in the opening game of Euro 96. Four games and four goals later and he was hailed as a marksman of proven international class for whom Newcastle were delighted to pay that then world record fee and bring Shearer home.

Now, with the World Cup in his sights, he has achieved another ambition after being appointed captain of England on Glenn Hoddle's managerial accession in 1996. And barring a recurrence of the type of injury which has kept Shearer out of action for much of the 1997–98 season, France will give him the perfect stage to prove his world-class credentials.

HRISTO STOICHKOV

His own man

Hristo Stoichkov is not only probably Bulgaria's greatest-ever player, he is also their most controversial. Stoichkov has been starring for his country ever since the mid-1980s. He was six-goal joint top scorer at the 1994 World Cup in the United States, where Bulgaria finished a best-ever fourth.

HRISTO STOICHKOV

Position: forward
Club: Barcelona (Spain)
Previous clubs: Maritza Plovdiv, Hebros Harmanli, CSKA Sofia, Barcelona (Spain), Parma (Italy)
Birthdate: February 8, 1966
Birthplace: Plovdiv
International appearances: 68
International goals: 35

"I'm a passionate person with all the accompanying virtues and defects but I've always done my best for every team I've played for"
– Stoichkov

But Stoichkov, fearlessly outspoken over the way the game is run, exploded in fury after the replacement of Dimitar Penev as national coach after Bulgaria's first round failure at the 1996 European Championship finals in England.

He staged a one-man protest boycott throughout the 1996–97 season, refusing to turn out for the national team despite being named repeatedly in the squad.

Stoichkov partly justified his stand by reference to the heavy programme faced by his Spanish club, Barcelona, in domestic league and cup and European Cup-winners Cup. Senior men in Bulgarian sport suggested that Stoichkov be disciplined for refusing to turn out for his country but new national boss Hristo Bonev struck a conciliatory tone.

Bonev had his own problems with authority in his playing days in the 1970s and he recognized the need for patience. In due course Bonev arranged peace talks and persuaded Stoichkov to bury the hachet for the World Cup qualifying run-in.

On June 8, 1997 – just over a year before the start of the World Cup finals – Stoichkov returned to duty after almost 12 months self-imposed exile. Luxembourg were Bulgaria's World Cup opponents in the provincial Bulgarian town of Bourgas. Appropriately, it was Stoichkov who achieved the breakthrough, scoring the first of Bulgaria's four goals just before half-time. He was back!

Stoichkov made his name with CSKA Sofia, the Bulgarian army team. He so impressed Barcelona in a European tie that they signed him, at coach Johan Cruyff's personal insistence, for a then Bulgarian record of £2 million in 1990. The relationship between the two men was stormy. Stoichkov scored more than 60 goals in his first three seasons in Catalonia but came close to the axe after transfer speculation on the eve of the 1992 Champions Cup Final.

The two patched up their differences and Stoichkov settled down to play the finest football of his career, culminating in the 1994 World Cup and his award as European Footballer of the Year. Stoichkov spent one season "away" at Parma before returning to Barcelona after Cruyff's departure, helping them win the Cup-winners Cup last year.

But, like Gheorghe Hagi, his fellow Balkan international and long-time friend, Stoichkov did not find Spanish football quite to his liking. That's why he will be fired up for the World Cup: he has enormous pride and an iron will to prove a lot of people wrong.

DAVOR SUKER

A leader on and off the field

Davor Suker knows all about international success. He won the 1987 World Youth Cup with the former Yugoslavia and has established himself, in Spain, as one of the most dangerous strikers in Europe.

"Lots of players have class. But ruthlessness in the penalty-box is rare. Suker has both – that's what makes him so dangerous"
– National coach Miroslav Blazevic

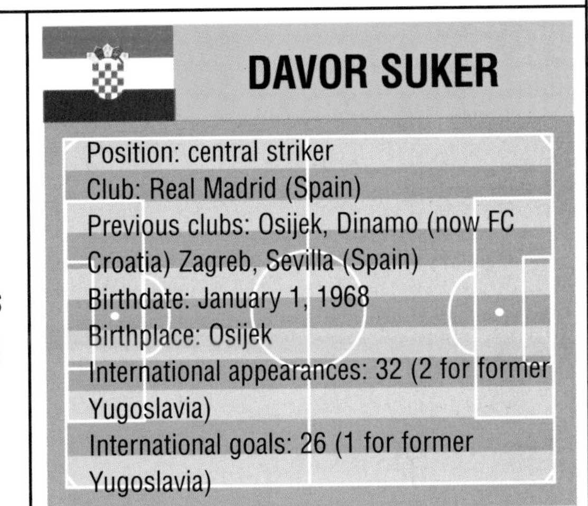

DAVOR SUKER

Position: central striker
Club: Real Madrid (Spain)
Previous clubs: Osijek, Dinamo (now FC Croatia) Zagreb, Sevilla (Spain)
Birthdate: January 1, 1968
Birthplace: Osijek
International appearances: 32 (2 for former Yugoslavia)
International goals: 26 (1 for former Yugoslavia)

Suker top-scored in the qualifying competition for Euro '96 with 10 goals as newcomers Croatia overcame Italy, Ukraine, Lithuania, Slovenia and Estonia. His razor-sharp talents in the penalty-box inspired a transfer auction two years ago when Real Madrid outbid competition from Bayern Munich and numerous Italian clubs for the Sevilla superstar.

What Madrid obtained – and what World Cup fans will see at France '98 – is a model footballer. Literally. Suker is a fashion freak. Like many high-profile celebrities he has a taste for Versace clothes and, because he is a man who knows what he wants and how to get it, Suker is the man who heads the Croatian players' negotiations on bonuses and sponsorship deals.

He says: "Footballers have a short career. It's a very public one. We are role models for young people but we also have responsibilities to our own families."

Croatia, both at the finals of the European Championship two years ago and now in their first-ever World Cup, also accept a responsibility to the people of their war-torn country.

Suker says: "We play, above all, for the people of Croatia. The federation has never had any money for big bonuses but that has never mattered to us. Our concern, since Croatia became independent, has been to give the people at home a reason to be proud. Something to provide them with a little happiness after all the troubles."

Suker, coach Miroslav Blazevic and team-mates Zvonimir Boban, Robert Prosinecki and Alen Boksic believe they can surprise the rest of Europe just as they did in 1996 when they reached the European Championship quarter-finals before losing a rugged duel by 2–1 to eventual winners Germany. Suker scored Croatia's goal after scoring two first round goals in the 3–0 victory over outgoing champions Denmark.

The Denmark match was one of the finest of Suker's career. His duel with goal-keeper Peter Schmeichel was a highlight of the finals – Suker getting the better of the Manchester United man with a beautiful chip for his second goal which left Schmeichel baffled.

Suker's past two years at Madrid have not been as straightforward as he had expected. In 1996–97 he found a hard task-master in Italian coach Fabio Capello, who expected Suker to track back. This past season he has had to fight off a challenge to his place from young Spaniard Fernando Morientes.

All the more reason for Suker to demonstrate his predatory nature in France.

TARIBO WEST

A star of Africa

When towering Nigerian defender Taribo West arrived – to his own surprise, as he has admitted – at Internazionale last year he was left in absolutely no doubt about his place among the superstars at the Italian Serie A club.

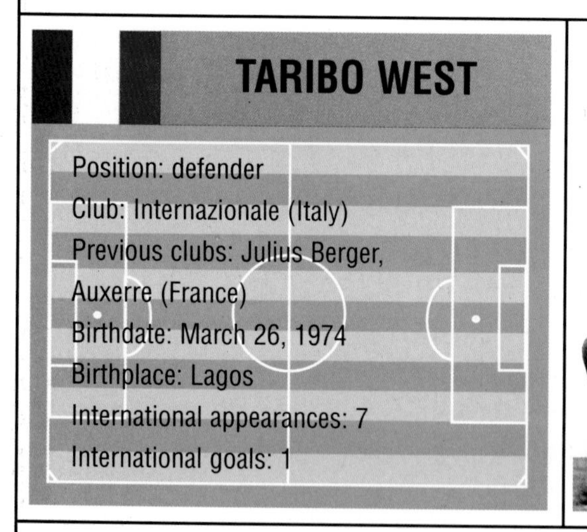

TARIBO WEST

Position: defender
Club: Internazionale (Italy)
Previous clubs: Julius Berger, Auxerre (France)
Birthdate: March 26, 1974
Birthplace: Lagos
International appearances: 7
International goals: 1

"I told the Auxerre coach [Guy Roux]: I'll not only be your best player but in a year or so you can sell me to a big Italian team and make a fortune"
– West

Inter's fans were also uncertain what to make of the new man. Crowds brought up on classical defenders such as the economical Armando Picchi, long-striding Giacinto Facchetti and iron-tackling Giuseppe Bergomi did not recognize West as a "typical" Inter player.

But his force of personality soon changed minds – just as he had previously won over all the scouts who had trodden a path to Auxerre to see the Nigerian man-mountain who was intimidating into anonymity all the best attackers in France's top division.

West, one of five boys born into poverty in Port Harcourt, had long dreamed of being a football star. As a kid he turned up each day at the Temporary Stadium, watching matches, watching training, kicking anything he could find.

"I wasn't one of those boys," he says, "who played just for fun. I always had ambition. They knew that. When I was a teenager the coach recommended me to a friend who ran a second division team in Lagos. He saw me play and told his directors: 'Taribo may not be very big but he has the heart of a lion.'"

Since those days West has developed a physique to match. He needed to know how to protect himself for he lived in one of the toughest quarters of Lagos. Ultimately the violence drove him back to Port Harcourt where he made his senior breakthrough with the local Sharks and then Enugu Rangers before transferring back to Lagos with top club Julius Berger.

West was tipped for a place in the national squad going to the 1992 African Nations Cup in Senegal. Nigeria won – but without him. Manager Clemens Westerhof thought him too young at just 18 years old and, anyway, he wanted only Europe-based professionals.

That was when West knew he, too, had to move to Europe. He did so in the spring of 1993, joining Auxerre. At first he was homesick. Not speaking a word of French did not help. But slowly West learned not only the language but the football as well, playing as he did alongside senior internationals such as Laurent Blanc.

In 1996 Auxerre shocked French football by winning the league and cup double. At the heart of defence was the giant figure of Taribo West. He was there for Nigeria, too, a few months later when they won the Olympic Games soccer tournament.

No wonder Nigeria qualified for the World Cup finals, where they are fancied to make serious progress. In France no one will strike fear into the opposition quite like Taribo West.

ZINEDINE ZIDANE

Following in giant boots

Zinedine Zidane is the new Platini for fans of Juventus – which is ironic since Platini is co-president of the organizing committee for the World Cup in which "Zizou" is needed to prove the point.

"Zidane is different class, even in such a remarkable team as Juventus. He plays off the ball as effectively as he does on it"

– Barcelona coach Louis Van Gaal

ZINEDINE ZIDANE

Position: midfielder
Club: Juventus (Italy)
Previous clubs: Cannes, Bordeaux
Birthdate: June 23, 1972
Birthplace: Marseille
International appearances: 28
International goals: 6

The 25-year-old midfielder who joined the Turin giants two years ago from French first division side Bordeaux has all the potential to succeed where even his hero could not – at the World Cup finals.

Zidane still half-believes he is dreaming. He says: "It seemed I had hardly arrived here in the summer of '96 and we were winning the World Club Cup. Then, another two months and we were winning the European Supercup. Fantastic.

"I had nearly said 'No' to Juventus. I had been tempted to stay at Bordeaux. I was happy. I enjoyed my football in France. The thought of playing in Italy was a little scary, a big challenge. But then I wanted to win the big prizes and I couldn't have done that staying in France."

Zidane, voted 1996 Player of the Year in France by his fellow professionals, was born in Marseille of Franco-Algerian origin. He made his top division debut for Cannes at 16 years of age, secured a big-money transfer to Bordeaux when he was barely 20 and marked his France debut two years later by scoring two goals after coming on as a substitute against the Czech Republic.

Fans abroad, struggling to remember his palid contribution to France's Euro 96 performances, may have been surprised at his emergence with Juventus. But fatigue induced by Bordeaux's Intertoto Cup campaign in the summer of 1995 – which led all the way to the 1996 UEFA Cup Final – had caught up with him.

Juventus's faith in the player never wavered, however. They had already deposited the first instalment of a £3 million transfer fee. Among disappointed competitors in the market were English champions Manchester United, who, a year later, lost their French playmaker Eric Cantona. But once Zidane had learned of Juventus's interest, that was the only foreign offer he would consider.

Following in the steps of Platini was too much of a temptation. Platini inspired France, as hosts, to win the European Championship in 1984. Zidane may hope to do as much at a "French" World Cup. If the curtain-raiser is anything to go by, Zidane will not spare any effort.

He was the European Select XI's finest player in the all-star match in Marseille, which was played immediately before the draw for the finals back in December and featured the best available players from each of the 32 countries qualifying for France '98. As Zidane said after the game: "I had to put in 101 per cent. After all, this is home."

That could be an omen.

WORLD CUP HISTORY

How the greatest competition in the football world began

A staggering 180 nations have taken part in the current World Cup but only 13 competed first time around, in Uruguay in July, 1930.

Despite being offered travel and accommodation expenses by the hosts, only four European countries dared the prospect of the three-week boat journey each way. England never even considered entering because they had walked out of FIFA – the international governing body – in 1927, in a dispute over expenses payments to amateurs.

The concept of a world championship was first raised in 1904 when FIFA was founded. At the time, most teams were amateurs and the Olympic Games winners were considered unofficial world champions. In 1924 and 1928 that meant Uruguay. But, as professionalism swept through European and South American football, FIFA recognized it was time to make the World Cup dream a reality.

At its 1928 congress, the president of FIFA, Jules Rimet, and the general-secretary of the French Football Association, Henri Delaunay, proposed a quadrennial championship, and French sculptor Albert Lafleur was commissioned to design a trophy.

The venue was decided at the following year's congress, one year ahead of the event and a far cry from the present procedure by which a host nation (or nations as in 2002) is nominated six years in advance.

Italy, Holland, Spain and Sweden all applied to stage the first finals but withdrew in favour of Uruguay, who aimed to celebrate 100 years of independence by welcoming the world and building a new 93,000-capacity stadium for the occasion.

But with two months to go, not one European nation had entered to join Uruguay, Argentina, Brazil, Paraguay, Peru, Chile, Bolivia and the United States. Angrily, the Latin American federations threatened to leave FIFA, and France, Belgium, Yugoslavia and Romania all relented and took part.

1930: The big kick off

The 13 teams were split into four groups, with Uruguay, Argentina, Brazil and the US the seeded nations. Four winners from these groups would advance to the semi-finals.

Uruguay score in the first World Cup Final – they eventually won

This hybrid combination of both league and knock-out formats shaped the pattern for future World Cups.

The finals were plagued with initial disappointments. The Centenario Stadium was not finished until five days into the tournament and crowds as low as 800 were turning up for matches. France beat Mexico 4–1 in the first World Cup game on July 13 before just 1,000 spectators.

The French were then defeated on the next matchday in a controversial game which was halted as they were about to equalize against Argentina. The Brazilian referee blew the full-time whistle six minutes early and players were leaving the pitch when he realised his mistake and called them back to restart the match.

It was too late for France, who sailed for home after losing the next game against Chile in a near-empty Centenario Stadium, which had been completed in time for Independence Day – July 18 – and 70,000 turned up to see the hosts struggle to beat Peru 1–0. Four days later the deciding game of the hosts' group was played before 80,000; Uruguay beat Romania 4–0 with all the goals coming in the first 35 minutes.

Top scorer in the tournament was Guillermo Stabile, known as El Infiltrador, who scored eight goals for Argentina, three of them in a 6–3 victory over Mexico, a game which had five penalties!

Argentina topped Group One, while Yugoslavia dispatched Brazil and Bolivia in Group Two. The big surprise was in Group Four, where the US reached the semi-finals without conceding a goal. Then, however, they proved no match for Argentina, who cruised into the Final 6–1 – the same margin by which Uruguay sent Yugoslavia packing.

The Final, a repeat of the 1928 Olympic final, was a true meeting of champions with Uruguay the Olympic gold medallists and Argentina the current South American title-holders. Not even England and Scotland – participants in the first ever international match in 1872 – had played each other as often as these neighbours.

The world's richest and most prestigious sports event attracted a crowd of only 1,000 for its launch 68 years ago.

Eager Argentine fans hired scores of boats to carry supporters on the short trip north across the River Plate from Buenos Aires to Montevideo. Tension was so high that all spectators were searched for firearms on their way into the stadium.

The Argentines were rewarded by seeing their team go into the second half leading 2–1 only for Uruguay to hit back to win 4–2. Captain Jose Nasazzi had the honour of lifting the world's most coveted trophy for the first time.

1934: Europe's first

Four years later Uruguay refused to defend their title – the only World Cup winners in history to do so. Upset that so few Europeans had taken part when they were hosts and plagued by players' strikes, they stayed at home. The 1930 runners-up, Argentina, took part but only grudgingly. They sent a team of reserves in protest at the way Italy, the host nation, had poached three of their best players. All had Italian parentage and one, Luis Monti, had played for Argentina in the Final in 1930.

When Italy manager Vittorio Pozzo was criticised for this, he retorted: "They are all eligible for national service here and if they can die for Italy, they can also play football for Italy."

Dictator Benito Mussolini saw the 1934 World Cup as a ideal opportunity for demonstrating the superiority of fascism. He told the president of the organising committee, Admiral Vaccaro: "Admiral, Italy will win the World Cup."

Vaccaro replied that, of course, everyone hoped the hosts would do well.

Mussolini said: "Admiral, I don't think you understood me. I said: Italy WILL win the World Cup..."

This time 32 nations took part – 22 from Europe, eight from the Americas and one each from Asia and Africa. A qualifying competition was necessary in which even the hosts were called upon to play, and won easily against Greece.

The British nations were still absent from FIFA and thus from the World Cup. Many felt England or Scotland would have won the competition but there was no doubt that the continental countries were narrowing the gap. England lost to Hungary and Czechoslovakia just before the World Cup began, and the Scots, on their last trip to the continent in 1931, had lost unconvincingly to Austria and Italy.

The tournament got under way on May 27, 1934. This time it was a simple knock-out event which meant that first-round losers including Brazil, Argentina and the US all went home after only one game – an 8,000-mile round trip for just 90 minutes' football.

Italy were probably the best team in the competition, but were helped by some lenient refereeing, particularly in the rugged quarter-final against Spain. In the semi-final Italy met Austria, probably the best team in continental Europe in the early 1930s, and won 1–0 with a 19th-minute goal from Argentine-born winger Enrico Guaita.

In Rome, in the other semi-final, Czechoslovakia scored an easy victory over Germany with a hat-trick from Oldrich Nejedly. The Germans' consolation was to beat Austria 3–2 in the first-ever third-place play-off.

Italy entered the Final as slight favourites but did not look it. With eight minutes remaining the Czechoslovaks led 1–0 and only a freakish goal from Raimundo Orsi pulled Italy level. Orsi, another Argentine, tried in vain to repeat the curling shot the following day for photographers but gave up after 50 attempts.

Angelo Schiavio scored the winner in extra time and Mussolini grinned triumphantly as he handed the cup to the Italian captain, goalkeeper Gianpiero Combi.

1938: Italy's double

The tensions which had built up through the first two World Cups rumbled on into 1938 when France were chosen, controversially, as hosts. The Cup should have alternated between South America and Europe but, at the 1936 FIFA congress in Berlin, France were chosen over Argentina. The South Americans refused to send a side for the next 20 years.

By the time of the finals Europe was in turmoil with the Spanish Civil War at its height and Austria swallowed up into Hitler's Greater Germany – who also took over the cream of their players. Austria already had qualified for the finals but no longer existed so, at short notice, England were invited to take part. They refused, and Sweden received a bye through the first round.

Uruguay again declined to enter and so the only Latin American contenders were Cuba, the Dutch East Indies and Brazil – with only the latter providing a serious challenge. It was the most unrepresentative of all the World Cups.

Once more, the format was all direct knock-out and Germany were surprise losers in the first round, going down in a replay to Switzerland. Also in the first round Brazil and

World Cup Legends: Combi

Gianpiero Combi (Italy):
Combi was goalkeeper and captain of the Italian team which won the 1934 World Cup. But his career had started in dire circumstances ten years earlier when he'd let in seven goals on his debut against Hungary. Italy's progress through to the final of the 1934 tournament was arduous in the extreme; a replay against Spain meant they played three matches in four days. Italy met Czechoslovakia in the final and only managed to beat them 2–1 in extra-time. Combi, playing in his 47th and last international, collected the trophy from Mussolini.

World Cup Legends: Meazza

Giuseppe Meazza (Italy):
Meazza was Italy's World Cup star of the 1930s. He arrived on the international stage in blazing style scoring two goals on his debut against Switzerland in 1930. When he retired in 1939 he had netted 33 goals in 53 matches. Along with inside-forward partner, Giovanni Ferrari, Meazza played in both the 1934 and 1938 Italian World Cup triumphs. Although Meazza didn't score in the 4–2 defeat of Hungary in the 1938 final, he scored the crucial penalty that knocked out Brazil in the semi-finals.

The World Cup survived two World Wars and saw Brazil become the most successful footballing nation the world has ever known.

Poland provided one of the most dramatic matches in the competition's history. Leonidas, the Black Diamond and the Pele of his day, scored four goals for Brazil, who won 6–5 in extra time. Poland's Ernst Willimowski also scored four goals... and still finished on the losing side!

Holders Italy beat hosts France in the quarter-finals, where Brazil also beat Czechoslovakia in a replay. The first match was the so-called Battle of Bordeaux, with two Brazilians and a Czech sent off, Nejedly breaking a leg and goalkeeper Frantisek Planicka suffering a broken arm.

Brazil paid the price for over-confidence in their semi-final against Italy. They rested Leonidas, to keep him fresh for the Final... which they never reached. Italy won 2–1 and qualified to face a Hungarian side who had thrashed Sweden 5–1 in the other semi-final.

Hungary played the better football in the Final but lacked the vital finishing punch. Italy led 3–1 at half-time and ran out 4–2 winners thanks to two goals from new centre-forward Silvio Piola and two by winger Gino Colaussi.

On hold for a decade

The Second World War halted all competitive football in Europe for the next eight years and FIFA could not give the World Cup even serious consideration again until its 1946 Congress in Luxembourg. Congress decided that the next tournament would be held in 1949, it would be renamed the World Championship, the trophy would be known as the Jules Rimet Cup after its creator... and the four British nations were welcomed back, along with the Soviet Union.

The priceless gold trophy had been kept safe during the war, hidden under the bed of the president of the Italian Federation!

1950: Uruguay Triumph

The first post-war World Cup was eventually deferred a year until 1950 and was awarded to the only applicants, Brazil. England took part for the first time while Uruguay, happy that the World Cup had finally returned to South America, competed for the first time in 20 years.

Brazil built a huge new stadium, the Maracana, with a 200,000 capacity, which was opened with a 21-gun salute and 4–0 win over Mexico. The format was switched to mini-leagues but the presence of only 13 finalists unbalanced the first round. One group comprised only two teams – and Uruguay qualified for the final mini-league merely by thrashing Bolivia 8–0.

Defending champions Italy, weakened by the loss of half-a-dozen top players in the Turin air crash the previous year, went out in the first round – as did England, shatteringly beaten 1–0 by the United States.

The result was so unexpected that some British newspapers listed the score as 10–1, convinced there had been a communications mistake. Haitian-born Larry Gaetjens scored the famous goal.

Brazil, Uruguay, Sweden and Spain qualified for the concluding group in which the last game, between hosts Brazil and Uruguay, was the effective Final. Brazil needed only a draw to become champions and 200,000 fans arrived in confident, carnival mood to witness the inevitable coronation.

Uruguay had other ideas. They survived the initial Brazilian attacking whirlwind and hit back to win 2–1 with goals from Juan Schiaffino and Alcides Ghiggia. Several shocked Brazilian fans died from heart attacks; others committed suicide.

1954: Hungary foiled

Switzerland, now the home of FIFA, were ideal hosts for the fifth World Cup in 1954. The format was changed again with first-round groups of four leading to knock-out quarter-finals and semi-finals.

Hungary, Olympic champions, were the hottest of favourites. In their opening two matches, against Korea and West Germany, they rammed home 17 goals. But the Germans had cynically fielded a team of reserves, confident that they could lose and still reach the quarter-finals – which they did after winning a play-off against Turkey.

The quarter-finals contained two games memorable for vastly different reasons – the match between Austria and Switzerland which produced 12 goals and the vicious Battle of Berne between Hungary and Brazil.

Austria beat their hosts 7–5 after having been 3–0 down in 23 minutes, while Hungary defeated Brazil 4–2. Three players were sent off and the match was followed by a mass brawl in the dressing room corridors.

By contrast, the semi-final between Uruguay and Hungary was considered to be one of the finest games of football ever played on the world stage. The Hungarians, undefeated since May 1950, won 4–2 in extra time, thanks to two headers from Sandor Kocsis.

As in 1950, the World Cup Final between the favourites Hungary and the no-hopers West Germany was considered a foregone conclusion. Hungary recalled skipper Ferenc Puskas, who had been injured against the Germans in the first round. Later it was suggested he was not ready and had been picked in expectation of merely having to carry off the cup.

Hungary stormed into a 2–0 lead – Puskas scoring one of them – within the first eight minutes. But by the sixteenth minute the Germans had pulled level. Right-winger Helmut Rahn then scored a shock winner late in the second half. Hungary had lost their first match in four years... the match which had mattered the most.

World Cup Legends: Schiaffino

Juan Schiaffino (Uruguay):
Schiaffino dreamed of being a centre-forward, but he was considered too frail for this position and so made his debut for Uruguay as an inside-forward. In the 1950 World Cup, Schiaffino scored a then record four goals in the 8–0 victory against Bolivia. He carried this rich vein of form into the final where he scored the equalizer against Brazil. Uruguay went on to win 2–1 in front of a record 200,000 fans.

World Cup Legends: Puskas

Ferenc Puskas (Hungary):
Puskas was the star player of the Hungarian side which dominated European football in the 1950s. Hungary started the 1954 finals in amazing style, beating South Korea 9–0 in their first match. But Puskas was affected in the later stages by injury, and even though he scored the opening goal in the final against West Germany, Hungary lost 3–2.

England finally become the top team in the world. But even they can't hold the title to the mighty Brazil.

1958/62: Brazil, Brazil

Not for 12 years would Europe celebrate another European success in the World Cup as Brazil, in both 1958 and 1962, produced the results which provided an overdue double reward for years of giving the world technically spectacular football.

Europe could not live with Brazil – and superstars such as Didi, Vava, Garrincha and, above all, Pele – in either 1958 or 1962. In 1958 Brazil became the first nation to win the World Cup in the "away" continent as they swatted hosts Sweden by 5–2 in the Final in Stockholm.

Pele, an amazing 17-year-old, scored twice in the Final – one the most cheeky of goals as he controlled a cross on a thigh, chipped over a defender's head and volleyed home from close range.

Four years later, in Chile, Czechoslovakia finished runners-up for a second time as they were rolled over 3–1 in Santiago. Czechoslovakia scored first in the Final through midfield general Josef Masopust but Brazil, even in the absence of the injured Pele, were on a different plane.

Europe's only consolation was that Frenchman Just Fontaine, in 1958, set a record which still stands by scoring 13 goals in the finals tournament.

World Cup Legends: Pele

Pele
Full name: **Edson Arantes do Nascimento** (Brazil)
The greatest player in the history of the World Cup. Pele starred at 17 in 1958, scoring twice in the Final victory over Sweden. Injury restricted him to two games in the victorious 1962 campaign and he was brutally kicked out of the 1966 finals. Returned in all his glory in 1970 to inspire Brazil's historic third World Cup win – scoring their opening goal in the 4–1 Final win over Italy. Pele played all his main club football with Santos, winning both the World Club Cup and the South American Club Cup (Copa Libertadores). In the mid-1970s he made a spectacular comeback with Cosmos of New York in the ill-fated North American Soccer League.

1966: Hurst's hat-trick

The World Cup returned to European hands in 1966 when England's 4–2 extra-time win over West Germany earned a knighthood for manager Alf Ramsey and places in legend for skipper Bobby Moore, Bobby Charlton and striker Geoff Hurst – the only man to have scored a World Cup Final hat-trick.

Yet England found goal-scoring tough in the first round, being held goalless in the Opening Match by Uruguay and beating

Martin Peters (extreme left) puts England 2–1 up against West Germany in the 1966 Final, the ball going between Karl Heinz Schnellinger (3) and goalkeeper Hans Tilkowski.

Having the best players and being favourites doesn't mean you will win a World Cup Final, as Holland found out in 1974.

World Cup Legends: Franz Beckenbauer

Franz Beckenbauer (West Germany)
The only man to have both captained and managed a World Cup-winning nation. He burst on the scene as a midfielder at the 1966 World Cup finals, helping West Germany finish runners-up and then third in 1970. Beckenbauer then switched back to bring a new, creative dimension to the role of sweeper and led the German hosts to World Cup victory in his home Munich Olympiastadion in 1974. Beckenbauer became the first German to top a century of caps (103) before winding down his career with Cosmos of New York and Hamburg. He managed West Germany to World Cup runners-up in 1986 and victory in 1990 before returning to Bayern Munich as, successively, director, coach and club president.

Mexico and France "only" 2–0 apiece. There were no such problems for West Germany. A brilliant youngster named Franz Beckenbauer inspired a five-goal show first time out against Switzerland.

Brazil were kicked out of the tournament by stop-at-nothing defenders from Bulgaria and Portugal, while Italy succumbed to a 1–0 upset at the hands of the mysterious North Koreans – who almost repeated the medicine against Portugal in the quarter-finals. Portugal went 3–0 down before recovering to win 5–3 and go on to achieve third place thanks to nine goals from Eusebio.

1970: Brazil again

Four years later, in Mexico, the Germans took dramatic revenge over England when they recovered from 2–0 down to beat – and eliminate – the holders by 3–2 in the quarter-finals. They then featured in an even greater contest which they lost eventually to Italy by 4–3. The Italians, mentally and physically drained, were then no match in the Final for Brazil, whose 4–1 win secured the first World Cup hat-trick. Even if fresh, Italy could probably not have coped with the brilliant Brazilians.

World Cup Legends: Johan Cruyff

Johan Cruyff (Holland)
Cruyff inspired not merely one country but an entire style change within football. He was the fulcrum around which Ajax Amsterdam and Holland developed the free-wheeling "total football." It brought Cruyff three European Champions Cups with Ajax, before he moved to Barcelona in 1973. It should also have brought World Cup glory a year later but Holland, despite being the darlings of the 1974 finals, lost 2–1 in the Final to West Germany. Cruyff led Holland back down the qualifying road in 1978 but then suddenly retired from the international scene before the finals in Argentina. Later he proved, with Ajax and Barcelona, to be as successful and innovative a coach as he had been a player.

Pele and the Jules Rimet Cup were a perfect match

1974: Dutch dismay

West Germany won on home soil in 1974 even though Holland – with their revolutionary total football – were, by general agreement, the finest of the contesting nations. English referee Jack Taylor awarded the first-ever Final penalty within two minutes of the kick-off in Munich. But West Germany, thanks to a penalty equalizer of their own and a typically

West Germany's Gerd Müller (front) and Paul Breitner celebrate victory in 1974

penalty equalizer of their own and a typically opportunist goal from Gerd Müller, won their second World Cup 20 years after the first.

1978: Hosts again

Argentina became, in 1978, the second straight host winners. Like West Germany four years earlier, they beat Holland in the Final – though the Argentines needed extra time and the intimidatory support of their fanatical fans.

Italy finished fourth and had the extra consolation of unearthing a new hero in quick-silver centre-forward Paolo Rossi – whose goals shot them to their own World Cup hat-trick in Spain in 1982.

1982: Three for Italy

Coach Enzo Bearzot took a huge gamble in 1982 by including Rossi, who had played only the final three games of the league season after a two-year ban for his alleged involvement in a match-fixing scandal. But he responded with a hat-trick in a marvellous 3–2 second-round defeat of Brazil and then the opening goal in the 3–1 win over West Germany in the Final in Madrid.

World Cup football then entered, for both better and worse, the era of Diego Maradona, the greatest natural talent since Pele. The youthful Maradona had savoured a tempestuous World Cup debut when he was sent off against Brazil in a group match in the 1982 finals. But his genius persuaded first Barcelona and then Napoli to pay world record transfer fees to bring him to Europe.

1986: Maradona

Every four years, of course, Maradona turned his back on Europe to lead Argentina at the World Cup. In 1986 that meant inspiring his country to victory in Mexico, albeit amid controversy. In the quarter-finals Maradona punched, against England, one of the most

World Cup Legends: Maradona

Diego Maradona (Argentina)
The most controversial – and uniquely talented – superstar of his era, Maradona, at 17, just missed a squad place at the 1978 World Cup and was sent off against Brazil when he did make the finals in 1982. World record fees of £3 and £5 million accompanied his transfers from Boca Juniors, via Barcelona to Napoli when Maradona dominated the 1986 World Cup. He not only captained Argentina to victory but scored twice against England, first one of the most controversial and then one of the most spectacular goals in the finals' history. The first was a clear handball, the other – two minutes later – a spectacular slalom from the halfway line. An injury-battered Maradona led Argentina to the runners-up spot in 1990 but he was sensationally expelled from the 1994 finals after failing a dope test.

World Cup Legends: Mario Kempes

Mario Kempes (Argentina):
Blooded in World Cup football terms during the 1974 tournament in Germany, Kempes was the finished article when Argentina hosted the finals four years later. He scored four goals in the early stages as he took his country to the final against Holland. On a night of great passion, Kempes scored two more goals as Argentina defeated the Dutch 3–1.

World Cup Legends: Paolo Rossi

Paolo Rossi (Italy):
Rossi went from national villain to hero in a matter of weeks during the 1982 finals. A star at the 1978 finals, Rossi was banned for two years in 1980 after becoming involved in a betting scandal. Only weeks after the ban ended, Rossi was back playing for Italy. He scored a superb hat-trick to send out Brazil in the quarter-finals, and then scored the opening goal in the 3–1 win against the Germans in the final.

Argentina won in Mexico in 1986 when Diego Maradona (10) proved his superstar status

Brazil again began to dominate the game again in the 1990s: the most expensive players and the best national team.

World Cup Legends: Dino Zoff

Dino Zoff (Italy)
Zoff became the oldest World Cup-winning captain when he led Italy to a surprise victory in Spain in 1982. By then he was 40 and well on his way to an Italian record 112 international appearances. Zoff played for Mantova, Napoli and Juventus in a remarkable career which brought him almost all the game's major prizes – starting at international level with the European Championship in 1968. Zoff eschewed flamboyance for an ice-cool security which inspired his fellow defenders. In 1982 he emulated another Juventus keeper, Gianpiero Combi, who had captained Italy to World Cup glory in 1934. After retiring Zoff found further success with Juventus as coach before moving to Lazio where he became, ultimately, chief executive.

Andreas Brehme (3) converts the penalty which won the Cup for Germany in 1990

the same match he displayed the other side of his talent by scoring one of the finest individual goals in World Cup history. In the Final against West Germany Maradona was well-policed by Lothar Matthäus. But when the Germans hit back twice in the closing stages to draw level at 2–2 it was Maradona whose pass sent away Jorge Burruchaga for the winner.

1990: That man again

Maradona also led Argentina to the Final in Italy four years later. Again they met a German team managed by Franz Beckenbauer with the World Cup at stake. But this was a mean-spirited Argentine side who played with a chip on their shoulder. Cameroon were the surprise force of the finals and only naivety cost them a 3–2 defeat by England in extra time in the quarter-finals.

England also were taken to extra time in the semi-final, by West Germany. The score was still 1–1 after the 120 minutes when Stuart Pearce and Chris Waddle missed the penalties which justified Paul Gascoigne's tears. Ironically, the Germans then went on to beat Argentina in the Final with a "real" penalty – converted by Andy Brehme after a trip on striker Rudi Völler.

World Cup Legends: Romario

Romario
Full name: **Romario de Souza Faria** (Brazil)
A winner's medal and the top player award were the dual prizes Romario seized at the 1994 World Cup. Initially, Brazilian coaches had despaired of integrating his gifted individualism into a team pattern. But goal-laden years in Europe with PSV Eindhoven and Barcelona added a gloss to his game. At the 1994 World Cup finals Romario contributed five goals to Brazil's run to the Final and then one of the shoot-out penalties in the dramatic climax against Italy. Romario's national team career went into decline as he went from Barcelona back to Flamengo and then back to Spain again with Valencia. But he regained his place at the Tournoi de France in June 1997.

1994: Brazilian record

Maradona grabbed the headlines again in the United States in 1994. The Americans were controversial but generously enthusiastic hosts. A clampdown on cynical time-wasting, the feigning of injury and the tackle from behind helped to provide a glorious advertisement for the game. Seven of the eight quarter-finalist nations were European. Only Brazil squeezed in among them on behalf of the rest of the world. Argentina had fallen to Romania in the second round, their spirit and morale punctured after Maradona had failed a dope test.

Europe's other contenders were Germany, Sweden, Holland, Bulgaria, Spain and Italy – and it was the Italians who faced Brazil in the Final. The goals of Roberto Baggio had brought Italy through but, when the Final ended goalless after extra time and was resolved for the first time by shoot-out, it was Baggio who missed the decisive penalty.

Brazil had won a record fourth World Cup and established themselves, beyond all question, as the world game's No. 1 – the team to be beaten...

Brazil receive the World Cup for the fourth time after defeating Italy in the 1994 Final

World Cup Finals 1930 – 1994

World Cup 1930 – Uruguay

SEMI-FINALS:
Uruguay 6 Yugoslavia 1;
Argentina 6 United States 1
FINAL: July 30 – Montevideo (Centenario)
Uruguay 4 (Dorado 12, Cea 58, Iriarte 68, Castro 89)
Argentina 2 (Peucelle 20, Stabile 37)
HT: 1–2. ***Att:*** 93,000. ***Ref:*** Langenus (Bel)
Uruguay: Ballestreros, Nasazzi, Mascheroni, Andrade, Fernandez, Gestido, Dorado, Scarone, Castro, Cea, Iriarte.
Argentina: Botazzo, Della Torre, Paternoster, J Evaristo, Monti, Suarez, Peucelle, Varallo, Stabile, Ferreyra, M Evaristo.
Third place: Not played.
Top scorer: Stabile (Arg) 8 goals.

World Cup 1934 – Italy

SEMI-FINALS:
Italy 1 Austria 0; Czechoslovakia 3 Germany 1
FINAL: June 10 – Rome (Flaminio)
Italy 2 (Orsi 81, Schiavio 95)
Czechoslovakia 1 (Puc 71)
(after extra time)
HT: 0–0. ***90min:*** 1–1. ***Att:*** 55,000.
Ref: Eklind (Swe)
Italy: Combi, Monzeglio, Allemandi, Ferraris, Monti, Bertolini, Guaita, Meazza, Schiavio, Ferrari, Orsi.
Czechoslovakia: Planicka, Zenisek, Ctyrocky, Kostalek, Cambal, Krcil, Junek, Svoboda, Sobotka, Nejedly, Puc.
Third place: Germany 3 Austria 2.
Top scorer: Nejedly (Cz) 5 goals.

World Cup 1938 – France

SEMI-FINALS:
Italy 2 Brazil 1; Hungary 5 Sweden 1
FINAL: June 19 – Paris (Colombes)
Italy 4 (Colaussi 5, 35, Piola 16, 82)
Hungary 2 (Titkos 7, Sarosi 70)
HT: 2–1. ***Att:*** 55,000. ***Ref:*** Capdeville (Fr)
Italy: Olivieri, Foni, Rava, Serantoni, Andreolo, Locatelli, Biavati, Meazza, Piola, Ferrari, Colaussi.
Hungary: Szabo, Polgar, Biro, Szalay, Szucs, Lazar, Sas, Vincze, Sarosi, Zsengeller, Titkos.
Third place: Brazil 4 Sweden 2.
Top scorer: Leonidas (Brz) 8 goals.

World Cup 1950 – Brazil

FINAL: July 16 – Rio de Janeiro (Maracana)
Uruguay 2 (Schiaffino 66, Ghiggia 79)
Brazil 1 (Friaca 48)
HT: 0–0. ***Att:*** 199,854. ***Ref:*** Reader (Eng)
Uruguay: Maspoli, M Gonzalez, Tejera, Gambetta, Varela, Andrade, Ghiggia, Perez, Miguez, Schiaffino, Moran.
Brazil: Barbosa, Augusto, Juvenal, Bauer, Danilo, Bigode, Friaca, Zizinho, Ademir, Jair, Chico.
Third place: Sweden (league format).
Top scorer: Ademir (Brz) 9 goals.

World Cup 1954 – Switzerland

SEMI-FINALS:
Hungary 4 Uruguay 2 aet;
West Germany 6 Austria 1
FINAL: July 4 – Berne (Wankdorf)
Germany 3 (Morlock 11, Rahn 16, 83)
Hungary 2 (Puskas 6, Czibor 8)
HT: 2–2. ***Att:*** 60,000. ***Ref:*** Ling (Eng)
Germany: Turek, Posipal, Kohlmeyer, Eckel, Liebrich, Mai, Rahn, Morlock, O Walter, F Walter, Schafer.
Hungary: Grosics, Buzansky, Lantos, Bozsik, Lorant, Zakarias, Czibor, Kocsis, Hidegkuti, Puskas, M Toth.
Third place: Austria 3 Uruguay 1.
Top scorer: Kocsis (Hun) 11 goals.

World Cup 1958 – Sweden

SEMI-FINALS:
Brazil 5 France 2;
Sweden 3 West Germany 1
FINAL: June 29 – Stockholm (Rasunda)
Brazil 5 (Vava 9, 32, Pele 55, 89, Zagallo 68)
Sweden 2 (Liedholm 4, Simonsson 80)
HT: 2–1. ***Att:*** 49,737. ***Ref:*** Guigue (Fr)
Brazil: Gilmar, D Santos, N Santos, Zito, Bellini, Orlando, Garrincha, Didi, Vava, Pele, Zagallo.
Sweden: Svensson, Bergmark, Axbom, Borjesson, Gustavsson, Parling, Hamrin, Gren, Simonsson, Liedholm, Skoglund.
Third place: France 6 West Germany 3.
Top scorer: Fontaine (Fr) 13 goals.

World Cup 1962 – Chile

SEMI-FINALS:
Brazil 4 Chile 2; Czechoslovakia 3 Yugoslavia 1
FINAL: June 17 – Santiago (Nacional)
Brazil 3 (Amarildo 18, Zito 69, Vava 77)
Czechoslovakia 1 (Masopust 16)
HT: 1–1. ***Att:*** 68,679. ***Ref:*** Latishev (SU)
Brazil: Gilmar, D Santos, N Santos, Zito, Mauro, Zozimo, Garrincha, Didi, Vava, Amarildo, Zagallo.
Czechoslovakia: Schroiff, Tichy, Novak, Pluskal, Popluhar, Masopust, Pospichal, Scherer, Kvasnak, Kadraba, Jelinek.
Third place: Chile 1 Yugoslavia 0.
Top scorers: V Ivanov (SU), L Sanchez (Ch), Garrincha, Vava (Brz), Albert (Hun), Jerkovic (Yug) 4 goals each.

World Cup 1966 – England

SEMI-FINALS:
England 2 Portugal 1;
West Germany 2 Soviet Union 1
FINAL: July 30 – Wembley
England 4 (Hurst 19, 100, 119, Peters 77)
West Germany 2 (Haller 13, Weber 89) (aet)
HT: 1–1. ***90min:*** 2–2. ***Att:*** 96,924.
Ref: Dienst (Swz)
England: Banks, Cohen, Wilson, Stiles, J Charlton, Moore, Ball, Hunt, B Charlton, Hurst, Peters.
W Germany: Tilkowski, Hottges, Schnellinger, Beckenbauer, Schulz, Weber, Haller, Overath, Seeler, Held, Emmerich.
Third place: Portugal 2 Soviet Union 1.
Top scorer: Eusebio (Por) 9 goals.

World Cup 1970 – Mexico

SEMI-FINALS:
Brazil 3 Uruguay 1;
Italy 4 West Germany 3 aet
FINAL: June 21 – Mexico City (Azteca)
Brazil 4 (Pele 18, Jairzinho 71, Gerson 66, Carlos Alberto 86)
Italy 1 (Boninsegna 37)
HT: 1–1. ***Att:*** 107,000. ***Ref:*** Glockner (EG)
Brazil: Felix, Carlos Alberto, Brito, Wilson Piazza, Everaldo, Clodoaldo, Gerson, Rivelino, Jairzinho, Tostao, Pele.
Italy: Albertosi, Burgnich, Cera, Rosato, Facchetti, Bertini (Juliano 75), Domenghini, De Sisti, Mazzola, Boninsegna (Rivera 84), Riva.
Third place: West Germany 1 Uruguay 0.
Top scorer: G Müller (WG) 10 goals.

World Cup 1974 – West Germany

FINAL: July 7 – Munich (Olympia)
West Germany 2 (Breitner 25pen, G Müller 43)
Holland 1 (Neeskens 2pen)
HT: 2–1. ***Att:*** 77,833. ***Ref:*** Taylor (Eng)
West Germany: Maier, Vogts, Schwarzenbeck, Beckenbauer, Breitner, Bonhof, U Hoeness, Overath, Grabowski, G Müller, Holzenbein.
Holland: Jongbloed, Suurbier, Rijsbergen (De Jong 69), Haan, Krol, Jansen, Van Hanegem, Neeskens, Rep, Cruyff, Rensenbrink (R Van de Kerkhof 46).
Third place: Poland 1 Brazil 0
Top scorer: Lato (Pol) 7 goals.

World Cup 1978 – Argentina

FINAL: June 25 – Buenos Aires (Monumental)
Argentina 3 (Kempes 37, 104, Bertoni 114)
Holland 1 (Nanninga 81) (after extra time)
HT: 1–0. ***90min:*** 1–1. ***Att:*** 77,260. ***Ref:*** Gonella (It)
Argentina: Fillol, Olguin, Galvan, Passarella, Tarantini, Ardiles (Larrosa 66), Gallego, Kempes, Bertoni, Luque, Ortiz (Houseman 75).
Holland: Jongbloed, Jansen (Suurbier 73), Brandts, Krol, Poortvliet, W Van de Kerkhof, Neeskens, Haan, R Van de Kerkhof, Rep (Nanninga 59), Rensenbrink.
Third place: Brazil 2 Italy 1.
Top scorer: Kempes (Arg) 6 goals.

World Cup 1982 – Spain

SEMI-FINALS:
Italy 2 Poland 0; West Germany 3 France 3 (W Germany 5–4 on penalties, aet)
FINAL: July 11 – Madrid (Bernabeu)
Italy 3 (Rossi 56, Tardelli 69, Altobelli 80)
West Germany 1 (Breitner 82)
HT: 0–0. ***Att:*** 90,000. ***Ref:*** Coelho (Brz)
Italy: Zoff, Bergomi, Collovati, Scirea, Gentile, Cabrini, Tardelli, Oriali, Conti, Rossi, Graziani (Altobelli 8; Causio 88).
W Germany: Schumacher, Kaltz, K Forster, B Forster, Stielike, Briegel, Dremmler (Hrubesch 63), Breitner, Rummenigge (H Muller 70), Fischer, Littbarski.
Third place: Poland 3 France 2.
Top scorer: Rossi (It) 6 goals.

World Cup 1986 – Mexico

SEMI-FINALS:
Argentina 2 Belgium 0;
West Germany 2 France 0
FINAL: June 29 – Mexico City (Azteca)
Argentina 3 (Brown 22, Valdano 56, Burruchaga 84)
West Germany 2 (Rummenigge 73, Völler 82)
HT: 1–0. ***Att:*** 114,590. ***Ref:*** Arppi Filho (Brz)
Argentina: Pumpido, Cuciuffo, Brown, Ruggeri, Giusti, Burruchaga (Trobbiani 89), Batista, Enrique, Olarticoechea, Maradona, Valdano.
West Germany: Schumacher, Berthold, Jakobs, K Forster, Briegel, Brehme, Matthäus, Magath (D Hoeness 63), Eder, Rummenigge, K Allofs (Völler 46).
Third place: France 4 Belgium 2.
Top scorer: Lineker (Eng) 6 goals.

World Cup 1990 – Italy

SEMI-FINALS:
West Germany 1 England 1
(West Germany 4–3 on penalties, aet);
Argentina 1 Italy 1
(Argentina 4–3 on penalties, aet)
FINAL: July 8 – Rome (Olimpico)
West Germany 1 (Brehme 84pen)
Argentina 0
HT: 0–0. ***Att:*** 73,603. ***Ref:*** Codesal (Mex)
W Germany: Illgner, Berthold (Reuter 74), Kohler, Augenthaler, Buchwald, Brehme, Hässler, Matthäus, Littbarski, Völler, Klinsmann.
Argentina: Goycochea, Lorenzo, Sensini, Serrizuela, Ruggeri (*Monzon 46), Simon, Jose Horacio Basualdo, Burruchaga (Calderon 53), Maradona, Troglio, *Dezotti.
*Monzon sent off, 65min; *Dezotti sent off, 86min.
Third place: Italy 2 England 1.
Top scorer: Schillaci (It) 6 goals.

World Cup 1994 – United States

SEMI-FINALS:
Brazil 1 Sweden 0; Italy 2 Bulgaria 1
FINAL: July 17 – Pasadena (Rose Bowl)
Brazil 0
Italy 0
Brazil 3–2 on penalties after extra time
Att: 94,000. Ref: Puhl (Hun)
Brazil: Taffarel, Jorginho (Cafu 21), Marcio Santos, Aldair, Branco, Mazinho, Mauro Silvo, Dunga, Zinho (Viola 106), Bebeto, Romario.
Italy: Pagliuca, Mussi (Apolloni 34), Maldini, Baresi, Benarrivo, Donadoni, Albertini, D Baggio (Evani 95), Berti, Massaro, R Baggio.
Third place: Sweden 4 Bulgaria 0.
Top scorers: Salenko (Rus), Stoichkov (Bul) 6 goals each.

FOOTIX'S FINAL WHISTLE

PICTURE ACKNOWLEDGEMENTS

The publishers would like to thank the following sources for their kind permission to reproduce the pictures in this book:

Allsport UK Ltd. 3, 37, 44t, 78b/Shaun Botterill 26t, 64, 71, Clive Brunskill 20, 21, 30, 35, Simon Bruty 7tl, David Cannon 78t, Graham
Chadwick 6, 12b, 53, Phil Cole 38, Michael King 77br, David Leah 23, 39, 43, 46, Clive Mason 29, Gary M. Prior 33t,b, 58, 68, Ben Radford 5tl,bl, 7tr,br,c, 18t,b, 36, 47, 56, 63, Mark Thompson 25t,b, Vandystadt/Stephane Kempinaire
26b, Frederic Nebinger 5r,
Allsport Historical Collection/Hulton Getty 75
Associated Press/Michael Lipchitz 12t
Colorsport 11br, 42, 55, 57
Empics 52, 59
The Football Archive/Peter Robinson 10l,r, 11t,bl, 13br, 50b
Robert Harding Picture Library 1
Mark Leech 44b, 51
Popperfoto 4l, 19, 22, 24, 27, 28, 31, 32, 34, 40, 41, 45, 49, 54, 60, 61, 65, 69, 70,
72, 76, 77t/Dave Joiner 8, McDermott 48, Reuters/John Kuntz 4r
Sporting Pictures (UK) Ltd. 62, 66, 67

Every effort has been made to acknowledge correctly and contact the source and/copyright holder of each picture, and Carlton Books Limited apologises for any unintentional errors or omissions which will be corrected in future editions of this book.

The time for talking is over. Thirty-two teams from all corners of the earth have gathered in France to battle it out for the right to call themselves football champions of the world.

Pre-match predictions will count for little out on the pitch. Instead it will be the team willing to chase every ball and make every tackle who will emerge triumphant. Teams will toil, sweat and shed tears in pursuit of victory. But only one side will lift the famous trophy. Who will it be? Not even Footix can tell you that!